BRIAN P. ZOELLNER

Learning Simulations in Education

NEW YORK AND LONDON

First published 2020
by Routledge
52 Vanderbilt Avenue, New York, NY 10017

and by Routledge
2 Park Square, Milton Park, Abingdon, Oxon, OX14 4RN

Routledge is an imprint of the Taylor & Francis Group, an informa business

© 2020 Taylor & Francis

The right of Brian P. Zoellner to be identified as author of this work has been asserted by him in accordance with sections 77 and 78 of the Copyright, Designs and Patents Act 1988.

All rights reserved. No part of this book may be reprinted or reproduced or utilised in any form or by any electronic, mechanical, or other means, now known or hereafter invented, including photocopying and recording, or in any information storage or retrieval system, without permission in writing from the publishers.

Trademark notice: Product or corporate names may be trademarks or registered trademarks, and are used only for identification and explanation without intent to infringe.

Library of Congress Cataloging-in-Publication Data
A catalog record for this book has been requested

ISBN: 978-0-367-17512-2 (hbk)
ISBN: 978-0-367-17514-6 (pbk)
ISBN: 978-0-429-05725-0 (ebk)

Typeset in Baskerville
by Apex CoVantage, LLC

Printed and bound by CPI Group (UK) Ltd, Croydon, CR0 4YY

Contents

Acknowledgements		vi
Preface		vii

One:	**Types and Theoretical Bases of Simulations**	1
Two:	**Learning Theories and Pedagogical Approaches to Simulations**	27
Three:	**Developmental Considerations of Simulations**	63
Four:	**Facilitating Cognitive and Metacognitive Processes during Simulations**	88
Five:	**Simulations in the Domains**	101

Glossary	126
Endnotes	130
Index	137

Acknowledgements

Many thanks go out to my colleagues at the University of North Florida College of Education and Human Services. The rich discussions around curriculum, teacher education, and learning provided important perspectives when considering the use of simulations in K-12 settings. Particularly helpful were the views of my non-STEM colleagues, as the humanities are not often associated with simulation technology. Another important influence for this project was my work with the Northeast Florida Center for STEM Education. Most specifically, I would like to thank Dan Dinsmore for his consistent collegiality and friendship. He was critical in the development of the concept for this book. I also want to thank Patricia A. Alexander and Daniel Schwartz for allowing me to be part of the Routledge Ed Pysch Insights Series. They have both been understanding and helpful throughout the process. Finally, I want to thank Nicole E. Rogers. Her feedback and support through this process were vital to the completion of this project.

Preface

> All around us people are learning with the aid of new technologies: Adolescents are playing complex, multi-player video games working in teams to achieve an objective, workers are interacting with simulations that put them in challenging situations, students are taking courses at online high schools and colleges, and adults are consulting Wikipedia to settle an argument. New technologies create learning opportunities that challenge traditional schools and colleges. These learning niches enable people of all ages to pursue an education or their interests on their own terms. People around the world are taking their education out of schools into homes, libraries, public wifi hotspots and workplaces, where they can decide what they want to learn, when they want to learn, and how they want to learn.
>
> (p. 1)[1]

For many years, different forms of educational technology have been promoted as a means to improve the quality of instruction, the accuracy of subject matter, and the increase of student engagement and learning performance. Historically, technologies such as films and videos have been used to make academic concepts more real and accessible to students sitting in a classroom. Like these instructional innovations, simulations, software or web-based applications that provide experiences that mimic the real world, can serve as mechanisms by which students can interact with phenomena that are often difficult to grasp because of the challenges of time or the limitations of size and scale. Simulations can also add authenticity by allowing students to examine data not normally available or ideas not usually feasible to explore in the typical classroom.

Much like the promoted instructional materials of the past, simulations hold much promise for use in K-12 classrooms; however, the real power comes from a deep understanding of the match between student interest and the need and function of these innovations. The innovations of the past—filmstrips, videos, laser discs—can be wonderful additions to the classroom but if educators do not find value in using these materials, they tend to sit on shelves collecting dust. Simulations must be seen as educational tools and, as such, connected to theories of learning, pedagogy, and instructional domains. Blind criticism or praise, which comes without consideration of how the technology can be effectively incorporated into the classroom, adds little value to the discussion. It would be akin to saying something like this: "a pencil harms learning history," or "the whiteboard promotes tremendous learning gains in English." As Gee noted when discussing games:

> [Game] players can be more or less reflective, strategic, and focused on game play rather than content or graphics. Critics of games need to consider how games are "consumed" by different people in different contexts. Blanket general claims (either for the good or the bad effects of games) are close to useless.
>
> (p. 198)[2]

What Gee observed about video games can also be applied to simulations. Without an understanding of instructional, learning, developmental, and curricular frameworks, the examination of the simulated experience boils to either being a booster or a curmudgeon.

PURPOSE OF THE BOOK

The book provides a synthesis and practical application of the use of learning simulations with students in K-12 education. While there has been varied scholarly work devoted to the effects of simulations, these volumes failed to comprehensively address the individual differences of prior knowledge, background, developmental level, and interests of learners and the contexts of simulation use including the academic domain and discipline and physical settings of different classrooms. This work addresses this critical gap with an accessible presentation of the psychological foundation of using simulations in teaching and learning and the specifics for application among diverse learners. In Chapters 1–4, the book introduces features of both the learner and the technology that are important to consider when using simulations in a variety of classroom situations.

In Chapter 5, the book explores applied settings—by academic domains and disciplines—and makes suggestions for specific simulations that might improve teaching and learning when applied to different topics. *Simulations in Education* is designed to be reader-friendly and includes a glossary of terms, along with explicit definitions of terms in the text and endnotes (rather than an abundance of internal citations). This book will serve to introduce new scholars to the psychological aspects of simulations and provide pre- and in-service teachers as well as the general public with a guiding framework for using simulations in the classroom to facilitate learning.

While there are examples of simulation use in informal settings, the primary focus of this book is to examine how simulations can work in school classrooms. Schools tend to be learning spaces that have clearer definitions of space and structure including curricular constraints around academic disciplines and age-specific student grouping. Informal settings are more variable, making it difficult to provide clear guidance to educators. That being said, some of the recommendations and findings delineated within may be useful in less formal learning environments. Simulation activities conducted at home, in museums, and in other learning venues may profit from an attention to the same learning frameworks, pedagogy, and developmental considerations.

WHOM THIS BOOK IS FOR

The book is intended to span two audiences. First, this volume may be useful for classroom educators, teacher educators, and beginning scholars who wish to better understand the psychological and pedagogical aspects of using simulations. The first four chapters of the book specifically address these concerns. This book may provide insight that would be useful for courses dealing with teacher educational methodology, educational psychology, or technology education. Specifically, this volume would serve as a valuable companion piece for courses examining learning theories and the role of simulations in learning.

Preface xi

The final chapter of the book, which addresses simulations in specific academic domains, will be most helpful for pre- and in-service teachers who would be interested in involving such technology in their classrooms and for experienced educators who desire more examples in doing same. Likewise, with an eye to addressing the needs of the broadest possible audience, the book will be written in an accessible manner. *Simulations in Education* will be both a valuable guide to using simulations effectively in the classroom and a key resource for teachers to select appropriate simulations.

A GUIDE TO THIS BOOK

Several techniques will be used to help the reader better understand the concepts and processes related to simulations. First, the book is organized into chapters designed with a focus on central issues and ideas related to using simulations in classrooms. This approach will consider how simulations integrate into effective learning frameworks and pedagogical practices, how developmental level is a factor when creating simulated experiences, how cognition and metacognition can be supported using simulations, and how they can foster domain-specific learning goals. Within these chapters, examples will be used to help ground the ideas in a pragmatic manner.

Second, endnotes at the end of the book are meant to help highlight examples of the key researchers and developers examining these issues and ideas. It is hoped that these resources will help make the material more accessible and useful to the intended audience. This bibliography is designed to be a "jumping-off" point to help readers begin their exploration of these topics. It can serve as a reading list and provide background in the key areas related to simulations used in educational settings.

Additionally, key terms will be bolded and defined within a glossary, which will serve not only to identify and build a dedicated vocabulary, but also to provide the reader a sense of how the field is defining these terms. Of course, some of these terms are evolving as the technology changes, but the glossary will provide some clarity for the purposes of this book. It is intended that these definitions will be grounded in both the theoretical and the applied aspects of simulations.

Finally, while the findings and conclusions within the book will be supported with the research of educational psychologists, technological experts and developers, domain-specific pedagogy experts, and curriculum analysts, it will also be designed to connect with the realities of simulation use in classrooms in the aim of meeting the needs of its audience. To help add clarity to these classroom applications, it will be noted when there are issues and considerations that are specific to each audience. Teachers and teacher educators should be able to glean insights into techniques and applications they can use to support learning in K-12 classrooms. It is also hoped that beginning scholars will find the book to be a primer addressing some of the key considerations when examining simulations. Ultimately, this book is meant to be a practical resource for both K-12 educators and early career graduate students.

WHAT THIS BOOK ISN'T

This book will not be a catalog of all current simulations available on the market. This decision was made for a few important reasons. Frankly, there are too many simulations to effectively vet and describe each one in this type of book. Much like any other technology, there are good simulations, bad ones, and everything in between. Sifting through the hype and the limited quality research examining the effectiveness of this technology is difficult and ultimately incomplete. Additionally, how one might evaluate these applications would vary in considering the goals of each domain and individual instructor. Also, the ever-changing nature of the landscape, with new and adapted applications rapidly rolling out to consumers, makes cataloging a daunting task. By the time this book is published, many new simulations will already be released, making it out of date almost immediately.

And the book is not a user's manual for individual simulations; it will not be focused on helping users with specific technical challenges (e.g., how do I get *Crystal Island* to work with my iPad?). Each simulation has its quirks and challenges, as do the various devices that will run the simulation. Additionally, there are lots of variations on the supporting platforms and nearly as many "hacks" to work through them. These topics may well warrant their own books. While there will be a general discussion of certain broad approaches and examples, each simulation has its own specific challenges and strengths for classroom use.

Because of these issues, it is more important for the reader to understand the general design of simulations. From this perspective, the reader can better determine how simulations can be applied to support existing frameworks of pedagogy and learning. In this application of the frameworks of teaching and learning, having a sense of the developmental and cognitive and metacognitive considerations is critical to the effective use of simulations. Having a better sense of these considerations will allow readers of this book to not only understand the use of existing simulations, but to also address emerging educational technologies or, to put it bluntly, to become more informed consumers. The hope is that readers can take what they learned from this book, develop an understanding of the simulation landscape, and make informed decisions when selecting the best application for their use or further study.

Brian P. Zoellner
Jacksonville, FL
September, 2019

One
Types and Theoretical Bases of Simulations

THE PROMISE AND THE PAYOUT

There are a number of advantages to using filmstrips and slides: (1) filmstrips are an excellent device for presenting close-ups of key steps involved in an otherwise difficult-to-view or dangerous process, (2) slides can serve that same function, but, additionally, are an excellent means of bringing a "field trip" into the classroom since they can be made by the teacher, (3) the order in which slides are presented is flexible, and individual slides can be removed easily and replaced with updated slides, (4) the equipment is portable, relatively inexpensive, and can be used in the average classroom as a part of normal classroom instruction, (5) these visuals allow students to see, as well as hear about, the material being covered, (6) students can be involved in the classroom activities by preparing slides or operating the equipment, and (7) students can use the equipment and materials on an individual basis. Filmstrips and slides can be used at any point in the lesson (introduction, body, summary), and they can be very effectively used in combination with other types of media such as the tape recorder.[3]

The quote above, found in an introduction to a manual on using filmstrips in classrooms, illustrates how various forms of educational technology have been promoted for many purposes and uses through the years. It might seem silly to begin a book about digital simulations with a vignette on filmstrips, but many of the reasons

2 Types and Theoretical Bases of Simulations

to use filmstrips in the classroom might be the same as those to use simulations. For example, simulations can allow students to do the following: change perspectives on difficult-to-observe phenomena, use different modalities to experience learning material, and be more engaged by putting themselves in control of the technology. Additionally, teachers can use simulations to take virtual field trips, and modify that experience to meet the needs and interests of students. The platforms and formats have evolved, but the educational technology promotion landscape has not changed a great deal. Compare it to the evolution of phone technology: What was once a communication device tethered to a wall is now a portable computer complete with a camera, a calculator, and a video game console, but at its base, it's still a phone. Punch in ten digits, and call your mom, dad, or caregiver. The latest simulation technology may look and operate differently, but the ways to consider its use in school remain constant.

Throughout history, technology has been an important part of the classroom. The advent of the overhead projector in the early 20th century allowed for reproduceable instructional practices through the implementation of re-usable transparencies. While ubiquitous today, the advent of the photo copier in the 1950s ushered in an age of rapid replication of materials, including news media. Film and video let instructors broaden their arsenal beyond static photographs and the printed word. And in the late 20th century, computers and the Internet further increased the type and amount of media available to teachers.

WHAT ARE DIGITAL SIMULATIONS AND HOW ARE THEY USED IN CLASSROOMS?

Simulations for educational use can take many forms. They are most often associated with computers, but historically physical and interpersonal activities have been considered simulations as well. For clarity, it is important to describe some of the kinds of simulations that exist. For example, there are differences between physical and digital simulations. **Physical simulations** are representations of systems or processes using objects or actions. These kinds of simulations have been used in the medical fields for a long time.[4] These applications of simulation technology tend to be scenario-based and have a focus on procedural learning outcomes. A common physical simulation used to foster the learning of a medical procedure is the Resusci Anne Simulator that is used to train medical staff and the public to conduct Cardiopulmonary Resuscitation or CPR.[5] Another example of a physical simulation might be an historical re-enactment of a Civil War battle. This scenario gives the participants and observers a sense, in a non-virtual space, what fighting in a 19th century theater of war might have looked, smelled, sounded, and felt like. Clearly the events are simulated, but many of the elements of war are present: smoke, cannon fire, troop maneuvers, and the like.

A **digital simulation** is defined as interactive software or web-based technology that provides students with experiences meant to mimic phenomena in the real world. Students interact with this technology by providing input (e.g., manipulating conditions, responding to a simulated action) while the simulation gives an output (e.g., change in conditions, movement and/or interaction between objects). For purposes of this book, we will confine our focus on digital simulations (for brevity, referred to as simulations moving forward in this book), although many aspects covered here can also apply to physical simulations. For example, simulations can help students develop a model for how they think the world works[6]; this objective can be applied to either form.

Interactivity describes the nature of both the inputs given by students (e.g., mouse, gesture-tracking software) and the outputs from the devices in response to these inputs. Outputs can include sounds, visuals, and haptics (e.g., vibrations, pulses). This immediate feedback provides the student an opportunity to influence the simulated environment in some way, perhaps to change a perspective (e.g., moving a sight line, or magnifying or shrinking objects), to manipulate an object (e.g., moving, separating, or combining objects), to speed up or slow down a process (e.g., change the time scale), or to ask for more information (e.g., help, create a data representation). Interactivity means simulated phenomena can be adjusted to make them more accessible to students; those changes to the elements with a simulation can include the following: 1) sped up or slowed down, 2) re-sized, 3) re-proportioned, and 4) important elements highlighted. With each of these modifications, the student can exert a level of control. For example, with the click of a mouse, the student can make items in the simulated environment grow larger or shrink, and either pick up the pace or apply the brakes to the action.

Simulations tend to be more virtual, although there may be physical elements used to interface with the simulation. **Input devices** allow the user to interact with the simulation in a tactile way; these devices can include a keyboard, mouse, and gesture-tracking devices. Lindgren, Tscholl, Wang, and Johnson categorized these inputs as low- and high-embodiment devices.[7] **Embodiment** refers to the nature and amount of movement required to provide input to the simulation. Low-embodiment devices would include a keyboard or a mouse, while high-embodiment devices would include motion-tracking devices.

Screen media is another term used to describe digital devices that often serve as input devices, such as touch screens. Screen media can be further divided into desktop and mobile hardware. In this categorization, mobile devices are those that can be more easily moved and manipulated (e.g., picked up, tilted, transported into various spaces) and include tablets and smart phones; desktop devices include those that are more place-bound (e.g., desktop computers). Traditional simulations are often designed for desktops and laptops. More and more mobile applications are emerging in the marketplace, but the research on them hasn't yet caught up with the pace of development. As a result, the greater focus of researchers is directed at place-bound hardware.[8]

Each screen medium has pros and cons. Lindgren et al. argued that the addition of kinesthetic action added a concrete nature to simulation activities that provided an opportunity for greater connection to abstract concepts.[7] Functions like "pinch to zoom" and "click and drag" technology in many touchscreens allow students to change the scale of what they are viewing in an intuitive manner. Some mobile hardware contains motion sensors that allow students the ability to provide input simply by moving the device. In this kind of hardware, input is given through **gesture-controlled interfaces**. These devices allow the user to physically act out the processes and relationships in a different, perhaps more intuitive, way than a mouse interface, with the hope of providing students a greater mental connection to the concepts being experienced.[7] However, tablet touch screens can require greater physical coordination, as students need to hold the device as they manipulate the images. These gesture-tracking devices often come at a higher cost than traditional desktop computers and monitors, which may make widespread use prohibitive.

The connection between the virtual and real spaces may have positive effects on student attitude by making the experience seem more concrete and meaningful. Consider a golf simulator as an example of a high-embodiment input device. The golfer swings a real club and drives a ball. Using sensors, the simulator determines the distance and direction of the ball as it heads into, ideally, a virtual fairway. The simulator is able to gather data on ball speed and location to simulate how the drive would behave on an actual golf course. Whether you can carry what you learn from the simulator into practice on the links is up to you; nevertheless, the experience of simulating your swing and getting data results internalizes the action of learning new techniques, all without having to rent a cart.

Types and Theoretical Bases of Simulations 7

Simulation outputs might include a screen from computer monitors, tablets, smartphones, and virtual reality headsets. Depending on the simulation, many elements might be part of the simulated experience: 1) animations, 2) raw numerical data, 3) data presented in multiple formats (e.g., graphs, tables), and 4) audio/video. These elements may serve as representations of real-world phenomena in a very close approximation, or be highly stylized so as to enhance a particular concept. Incorporating these elements can be important when engaging students, as Squire, Barnett, Grant and Higginbotham noted when using a simulation to teach about electrostatics: "as *representations* of electrostatic ideas, animations and visual depictions are not only tools for thinking about physics but objects that can engage, excite, and inspire learning" (p. 515).[9]

Simulated outputs might also include projected images incorporated into the motion-capture process; often these images are used to more closely mimic what they are representing. Again, think of the golf simulator: The projected image is that of a golf course, designed to simulate playing a game on an actual course. Another simulation might be one that helps train police officers in how to react to dangerous situations. These formats may incorporate a simulated device—a golf club, a gun, or a steering wheel, perhaps—to capture the participant's motions that are then transferred into the projected images that suit the particular situation—traffic, a dark alley, or the ninth hole.

Other examples of simulated outputs can be viewed through portable devices designed to be worn. These devices are most closely associated with augmented reality, a type of simulation that serves as a blend of reality and an added component. This interface may be useful in the social studies field to simulate historical events or settings; the interface also allows for multi-person interaction. This **mediated emersion** allows students to work within an all-encompassing, digitally enhanced environment.[10] These enhancing components could include text information about a location, details of images as seen through the viewer, etc. Global Positioning Systems (GPS) within these devices allow the platform to gather location information and enhance the experience based on this context. For example, imagine a student moves to an historically significant site on a battlefield. The device would sense the student's exact location, and provide additional information via audio, video, or text that would not normally be immediately on hand in reality. Clothing enabled to capture movement, including bodysuits, gloves, and helmets, can be used as simulation hardware, as well; they can provide both inputs and outputs to the wearer. For example, virtual-reality helmets can offer a more immersive experience for the user. In addition to light and sound, haptics—physical feedback such as vibrations or pulses—and moving air can become part of the experience for students. Adding to the richness of these outputs, the *FeelReel* virtual-reality device can simulate wind and scents.[11]

In addition to the hardware and output devices, a better understanding of the nature of simulations requires a sense of the functions they provide. These categories tend not to be discrete, though; some simulations may have functionalities that cross multiple categories. The first is a simulation of a setting. For example, students may work in a simulated scientific lab, where they may be provided structure to engage in scientific processes like laboratory experimentation, data collection and analysis, and formation of steps to help develop sound conclusions. Within this setting, a narrative may be added to give context to engage students, keep them focused, and provide a structure to help them through the investigative process.[12] In other settings, students may engage in creating a city where they have to consider how best to support citizens in a sustainable way. In these simulations, students may adopt an approximation of a professional role (e.g., historian, mayor, chemist), but each setting dictates a measure of authenticity meant to simulate the real-world functions and the defined objectives of that role.

A second category of simulation function is that of phenomena. In this type, students can experience a mimic of something that exists in the world but is difficult to access either because of the limitations of a classroom setting or the various developmental levels of the students. These simulations may include simplified versions of phenomena, which may include representational models of photosynthesis by showing idealized and enlarged leaf structures and cells to show the locations of important reactions. They can also provide safer experiences by allowing students to virtually work with radioactive, flammable, and explosive materials. Simulations may also change the time scale of normally slow phenomena (e.g., evolution of a city in hours instead of years) or slow down rapidly developing processes (e.g., radioactive decay) to make these concepts more accessible to students. Relatedly, simulations can also provide time- and size-scaled representations, as in the case of sped-up versions of mitosis and cell division. These phenomenological outputs might support students to more easily visualize concepts that may be hard to grasp by providing the modeling of objects, visual labs, interpersonal games, and data generation.

The nature of simulations can vary widely, affecting how they can be used in classrooms. While some of simulations are highly structured, and the user experience is controlled by developers, others allow for instructors to make modification and exert control over what can be viewed by students. In cases where there is no existing simulation for a particular phenomenon, some instructors have designed their own. Existing platforms can be so modified, as Frederking did when he used a course-management platform (Blackboard) to create his simulation in political science.[13] As another example, Fraser, Pillay, Tjatindi, and Case created their own simulation using Microsoft Excel to support college engineering students in understanding fluid dynamics—more specifically, concepts related to pressure measurement, the flow of fluid through pipes of varying diameters, and fluid behavior between two plates.[14]

Simulations also allow for experiences that might be logistically difficult to provide because of concerns regarding safety, budget, or classroom management concerns. For example, providing students the opportunity to experience trench warfare might give them a first-person prospective for a better context into Erich Maria Remarque's *All Quiet on the Western Front,* but this presents several obvious issues that simulations can solve. The first obvious issue is safety. Even if there were an accessible trench war in modern times that could serve as an analogy, it is a very bad idea to put students into an active war zone. Next, even if there were a safe way to bring students to said war zone, it would be costly in both time and money. The third issue is a temporal problem. As World War I is historical, students cannot observe it first-hand. Finally, if all the other issues were addressed, there is little structure to help students observe and take note of the most important observations. Simulations can address all of these challenges.

Digital games provide a unique category of instructional technology and are defined by Halverson and Steinkuehler as those programs that are

> interactive and involve some form of problem solving: the player is given a goal of some form that does not match their current state and must overcome obstacles to accomplish the goal.
>
> (p. 376)[15]

Games typically have rules and parameters, require the user to work toward achieving an outcome, and provide status reports on progress toward this outcome. They are often used in informal settings and are often highly engaging to the user. Many games, if they mimic natural or human-made phenomena, can be considered simulations. An example might include *SimCity*, where the player assumes the role of a city planner, while trying to achieve a goal set by the user (e.g., to maximize wealth or to increase the well-being of citizens).

Types and Theoretical Bases of Simulations

One might be tempted to categorize games outside the purview of an examination of simulations, especially since they are often used in informal settings. However, they share some important characteristics as noted by the National Research Council:

> Simulations and games lie along a continuum, sharing several important characteristics. Both are based on computer models that simulate natural, engineered, or invented phenomena. Most games are built on simulations, incorporating them as part of their basic architecture.
>
> (p. 8)[16]

This view that some games can be considered simulations is also supported by Gee, as he noted:

> However, the video games in which we are interested here—for example, in the case of commercial games, games like *Deus Ex*, *Half-Life*, *The Sims*, *Rise of Nations*, *SWAT IV*, *Civilization*, *The Elder Scrolls III: Morrowind*—are, indeed, simulations. They are worlds in which variables interact through time. What makes them interestingly different from scientific simulations is that the player is not outside, but, rather, inside the simulation (the virtual world). There are also cases like flight simulators and games like *Full Spectrum Warrior* which are used, in one form, as professional training devices and, in another form, as games for the commercial market.
>
> (p. 199)[2]

Since games are built upon a representation of phenomena, they can be considered part of the simulation constellation. Games can be useful in educational settings even if they are not as integral to the curriculum, as this view from Richard Halverson and Constance Steinkuehler indicated:

> [E]ven games whose content is not overtly educational can, and frequently do, require intellectual practices that result in educational outcomes as a by-product of the basic problem solving that is required within any title.
>
> (p. 377)[15]

To keep with the focus of this book, games that can be used to represent phenomena in the real-world and are used within the typical K-12 curriculum and classroom setting will be examined as a category of simulations or game-based simulations. The experiences can be shared among students, from which teachers can draw lessons. Students are very interested in these types of applications, and that can help with motivation. Using games can tap into this excitement, and it can help to provide experiences that simulate real-world scenarios and human interactions. These utilizations may, in turn, foster teamwork, learning and following procedures, and (virtual) interpersonal skills.[15]

In addition to games, some virtual reality applications can be considered to have a simulation component. Rubio-Tamayo, Barrio, and García García categorized virtual reality into those with artificial, simulated, and alternate realities.[11] They noted the uses of virtual reality in multiple settings, including education:

> Virtual reality has also been a medium used in the development of training systems, due to its power of simulation.

Types and Theoretical Bases of Simulations

> The relationship between simulation, interactivity, visual representation and training makes virtual reality a relevant research field. Virtual reality is then applied not only to science dissemination and communication, among other things, but also as a medium for developing safe environments for practice in some research disciplines, due to its interactive potential with the environment.
>
> (p. 7)

However, like games, not all virtual reality experiences can be considered digital simulations for educational use. For purposes of this book, we will consider only those virtual reality simulations that can be connected explicitly to curriculum standards and teaching objectives. Those virtual reality applications focused on scientific exploration and communication will not be addressed in this space.

When discussing digital simulations, we may be talking about **augmented reality** or **mixed reality** applications—simulations that incorporate some real-world aspects (e.g., movement in physical space, a connection to a specific location, enhanced images), while providing various simulated aspects (e.g., illustrated characters or objects, information, modification of real-world images). **Virtual reality** applications are more immersive and are completely separated from the real-world. **Whole body** simulations allow the user to create movement while learning about phenomena. An example of a whole body, mixed-reality simulation game is *MEteor*, a simulation about motions of celestial objects that utilizes the entire classroom with laser-based motion tracking designed for secondary students.[7] One task

Types and Theoretical Bases of Simulations 15

in this simulation asks students to make predictions about the trajectory of an asteroid as it approaches a planet; they are then able to judge the accuracy of their predictions through the simulation. As an example of student movement, students test their predictions by moving to place meteors in virtual launchers and step forward to initiate a launch. This simulation experience is more immersive than others that only use a desktop computer and mouse; real-time feedback, in the form of instructions, data, and information on positioning, is projected onto the wall and floor of the simulated environment, not limited to the (relatively) small space of a computer monitor's screen.

The hardware that simulations use is varied and constantly evolving. The main platforms can range from desktops to cellular phones, and incorporate peripherals including headwear and electronic pencils. Again, the purpose here is not to catalog all of these specific devices and models; indeed, that list would likely be out of date by the time this book is published. What we will do, however, is describe the general functionality and use of these items. In many cases, simulations are viewed using a screen, be it on a computer monitor, a tablet, or a phone; however, when appropriate, it will be noted when a specific type of hardware excels at enhancing the particular features of a specific type of simulation. A tablet, with its portability and easily viewable screen, might be the best option for students when working with an augmented reality application with simulated events that can be found at historical locations. Or wearable headgear could be the right choice when immersion in an environment is key, such as when using

Types and Theoretical Bases of Simulations

a simulation that allows students to feel as though they are inside an electrical field.

One way to organize the myriad devices and peripheral is to describe whether they are portable or require a fixed station. Klopfer, Squire, and Jenkins described some of the key functions of Personal Digital Assistants, though these functions also apply to smartphones and many tablets:

- *portability*—can take the computer to different sites and move around within a site
- *social interactivity*—can exchange data and collaborate with other people face to face
- *context sensitivity*—can gather data unique to the current location, environment, and time, including both real and simulated data
- *connectivity*—can connect handhelds to data collection devices, other handhelds, and to a common network that creates a true shared environment
- *individuality*—can provide unique scaffolding that is customized to the individual's path of investigation. (p. 95)[12]

WHY USE SIMULATIONS?

Simulations can be useful to educators for multiple reasons. The first is logistical—price, safety, and time are all factors that can be addressed by using simulations instead of real-world experiences. In looking at science activities, Scalise, Timms, Moorjani, Clark, Hoffermann, and Irvin discussed some of the background challenges that administrators must address when they make decisions about simulations:

Types and Theoretical Bases of Simulations

> Providing students with the most effective teaching method may be paramount, but today's realities add growing weight to other criteria: the high cost of lab equipment and materials; the inflexibility of dedicated, single-use school space for hands-on labs; the potential dangers and liabilities of using chemicals, tools, and other lab materials; the use of precious classroom hours to set-up traditional experiments, sometimes repeatedly to gather comparative data; and the heightened student sensitivity to ethical questions of experiments that, for instance, use real animals or are not environmentally "green."
>
> (p. 1051)[17]

Cost, both in terms of money and time, is a major logistical factor when deciding whether to use simulations. Field trips can be expensive and difficult to manage within a close proximity to school (e.g., trips to the local museum, aquarium, zoo), and experiences in other states or countries can be prohibitive. Augmented reality simulations can allow students the opportunity to experience unfamiliar, even exotic, locations for the cost of the simulation. Costs of materials for labs can also be expensive; consumable chemicals are one aspect, but equipped rooms, experimental apparatus, safety equipment, storage space, and proper disposal procedures only add to the substantial overhead costs. Using simulations sets aside the expertise and oversight necessary to properly maintain these materials and facilities and lets educators focus on instruction.

While logistical considerations are important and can provide a strong case for using simulations, it might be more useful to examine the strengths of simulations

Types and Theoretical Bases of Simulations

from a more curriculum and instruction perspective, as these considerations speak more directly to the needs and interests of students. Simulations can be useful in helping students grasp difficult concepts:

> Simulations allow users to observe and interact with representations of processes that would otherwise be invisible. These features make simulations valuable for understanding and predicting the behavior of a variety of phenomena, ranging from financial markets to population growth and food production.
>
> (p. 9)[16]

From a curricular and pedagogical standpoint, simulations can provide advantages over traditional classroom practices; simulations might offer material that is dynamic and responsive to students' needs and interests. When compared to traditional curricula like print media, students can provide input that garners immediate and individualized response that just won't come from static words on a page. For example, in a climate change simulation, students might manipulate the level of forested land and observe the projected carbon dioxide levels in the atmosphere over time; another manipulation would yield a different set of projections:

> For example, dynamic visualizations may improve learning by illustrating abstract time-dependent concepts, by simulating complex system behavior, by demonstrating sequential processes, and by focusing and guiding the learners' attention
>
> (p. 326)[18]

Types and Theoretical Bases of Simulations 19

Having this kind of control allows students to more actively see how changes in conditions can cause outcomes on a global scale, allowing students to explore in a way not normally accessible within the limitations of a traditional curriculum.

Simulations also allow students to manipulate phenomena that typically would not be feasible to modify in real space, maybe because of the size of the system they are examining. Say, for example, the lesson calls for changing abiotic variables within a watershed to see how biotic components of the ecosystem are affected. This action would be very difficult to perform in real space for a few considerations: the size of the watershed, the logistics of making these changes, the ethical conundrums of changing the ecosystem for the worse, and the time it would take to collect the data and, perhaps, run the experiment again to check the results.

Simulations can create a low-risk space for students to make mistakes and examine their choices. There are times when educators want students to try new things, experiment, test ideas, and challenge their thinking. Time, safety, and material costs raise the risks for teachers to try this more open-ended approach to instruction; simulated options that provide educators that option might include interactional games (e.g., *SimCity*) or virtual laboratories (e.g., *PhET* lab simulations). The risks for safety, both emotional and physical, and the costs of time to set up, run, and re-try labs, are minimized using simulations, since actual materials or facilities are not a factor. Time and materials are not wasted, so there is less risk in messing up both in terms of messy data and messy lab stations. When working with college-aged physics students, Adams found that students who worked with simulated circuit labs performed better on assessments of their understanding of circuits and were more comfortable when they worked with actual materials on a follow-up lab activity when compared to students who strictly used real-world equipment.[19]

Simulations are also interactive, which may aid in student learning.[20] This interactivity can include user control, dynamic feedback, and differing representations of phenomena[19], which might include those with macroscopic and microscopic views, those represented by mathematical equations and graphs, and those that feature animations.

Additionally, simulations allow the instructor to provide context with major concepts of the domain. Experiences can be situated in a manner that allows students to imitate how knowledge is generated in a particular field. For example, students can engage in the simulated experiences of an historian by examining and analyzing authentic artifacts. They can then record observations, and perhaps even draw conclusions from their work, mirroring what real historians might do.

Finally, recent shifts in national focus and standards may make simulations more valuable. When speaking about games, the points Halverson and Steinkuehler make about their supporting many of the learning goals described by the national educational reform documents could apply to simulations in general:

> Moreover, the standards for what counts as successful learning are rapidly evolving.
>
> Initiatives such as the *Common Core State Standards Initiative*, the *Partnership for 21st Century Skills* and the *Next*

Types and Theoretical Bases of Simulations 21

Generation Science Standards are moving away from traditional measures of content mastery and toward performance-based standards that require learners to express learning through production and participation in meaningful situations. For educators struggling to adjust traditional instructional programs and practices to meet these new expectations for learning, video games and the worlds around game play provide robust and well-tested examples of how learning might be coordinated in online and in-person environments.

(pp. 377–378)[15]

Simulations can function as a valuable resource for teachers needing to adjust their pedagogical practices to better address performance-based standards.

WHAT ARE SOME KEY CONSIDERATIONS FOR WORKING WITH SIMULATIONS?

There are multiple factors to consider when choosing to use a simulation, selecting which product to use, and understanding how to use it. The first consideration relates to pedagogy: how do simulations fit within and support pedagogical frameworks? The second facet is student-centered: how best to ensure the simulation is appropriate for the developmental level of the student. How simulations support metacognition forms the third point that should be considered. Here it is important to examine the processes and strategies that may be facilitated through the use of simulations and how these processes may lead to more desirable learning outcomes. The final consideration relates to the differences in simulation use across the domains. The field of study—science, social studies, what have you—dictates which simulation is selected and how it is used by the teacher.

The caveat, as always, is that these technologies may be poorly integrated into instruction or support existing practices that fail to improve student outcomes. Much like other technologies promoted for educational use, there has been much support for the application of simulations for the classroom; however, the manner in which they are put into practice affect how successful they will be. Merely sitting students in front of a computer will not necessarily maximize the effects that simulations can have. Teachers need support from the technical side (to answer questions such as: What happens when the simulation crashes? Or: How do I get it to work with a Mac?), as well as from the application side (to address concerns such as: How do I get the software to show a graph? Or: How can I monitor the chat space?). Additionally, time must be spent finding ways to integrate simulations into pedagogical frameworks and curricula. Bringing the applications into the classroom is just the beginning of the process of utilizing simulations effectively.

Even while schools and districts may choose to use simulations as a way to cut costs, as noted in the previous section, the accompanying equipment still can be expensive to buy, maintain, and update. Bring Your Own Device may be an option to defray both the cost to schools as well as the learning time required to understand and operate the technology. But consideration must be paid regarding access to the devices and to sufficient networking capabilities; for some students, acquiring equipment may be a hardship. Ultimately, though, the software and hardware may only amount to a small portion of the fiscal cost of bringing simulations to the classroom; professional development and support may present a much higher cost in both money and time. As with many new techniques and technologies applied to the classroom, ongoing professional development is critical in regards to simulations.[10] One-day workshops about these new applications is a start, but that alone may not be effective to insure their successful implementation. The need for ongoing support is vital for instructional technology, but especially pressing for a continually developing field such as simulations.

As with many promoted "advances" in education, moderation, balance, and levity are often good mindsets to have toward new approaches, and simulations are no different. While simulations may serve to address a specific niche in classrooms and labs, they cannot completely supplant good teaching practice. The emerging evidence suggests that while this technology can help students experience simulated phenomena not normally accessible in a typical educational setting, it is enhanced by supplemental instructional practices by the teacher, including introducing the simulation, questioning the students during their work, and debriefing with the class after the activity.[20]

ORGANIZATION OF THE BOOK

In their examination of the educational game literature, Miller and Kocurek proposed five principles in application design:

> That is, we argue educational games should: (1) have developmentally appropriate content, (2) integrate the

theoretical frameworks from learning sciences, (3) embed learning in socially rich contexts, (4) develop diverse content, and (5) create a balance between play and real-world learning opportunities.

(p. 315)[21]

Again, though the authors were speaking with an eye toward games, these principles can yet be useful in examining the broader use of simulations in classrooms, as much of the technological and hardware considerations overlap.

de Freitas and Oliver, in their review of the literature, outlined several key considerations when examining the use of simulations.[22] Their review helped inform the focus and organization of this book. One consideration centers on the **processes of learning,** both during the course of formal curricula-based learning time and during informal learning: "In particular this dimension promotes the practitioners' reflection upon methods, theories, models and frameworks used to support learning practice" (p. 254). This concept connects to Miller and Kocurek's notion of tying digital applications to the learning sciences, and the integration of the two will serve as the focus of Chapter 2, which includes a treatment of the relationships between simulations and learning frameworks. Chapter 2 will offer practical advice about how to implement simulations within a classroom setting, including how to support their use through student-centered pedagogical strategies, those that are inquiry-oriented and constructivist. These strategies will be designed to support not only the development of understanding the subject matter,

Types and Theoretical Bases of Simulations 25

but also the processes important in knowledge generation across multiple disciplinary domains. Additionally, Chapter 2 will connect these theoretical perspectives to pedagogical approaches to ways that make these frameworks more practical.

In a second consideration, de Freitas & Oliver focused upon considerations about the **learner and classes**. They included age, grade and developmental level, and learning background and preferences. These aspects address the developmentally appropriate and diverse content described above.[22] Chapters 3 and 4 describe the critical developmental considerations when using simulations.

In the third chapter, developmental considerations around simulations will be discussed. These include critical differences in substance, along with recommendations about how to approach supporting students of differing ages and developmental levels. While the selection of the appropriate simulation will be important, teaching approaches and instructional supports are also critical when considering the developmental level of the students working with the simulation.

Cognitive processing is the focus of Chapter 4, especially how simulations allow students to use reflection to support metacognitive development. Deep understanding of unfamiliar phenomena requires students to make sense of their experiences with them. This process can be fostered through simulations by providing scaffolded learning through instructional procedures and tailoring experiences to the needs and interests of the students. This chapter will discuss important considerations to maximize these cognitive and metacognitive processes.

A third consideration focuses on the internal **representational world**—or diegesis—of the game or simulation, which in this context is used to mean the following: the mode of presentation, the interactivity, and the levels of immersion and fidelity used in the game or simulation[22]. Making the connection between play, the real world, and the socially rich contexts can be a domain-specific dimension and is addressed in Chapter 5. Finally, differences among simulations across domains will be discussed in Chapter 5, particularly how simulations provide access to phenomena not normally available to students. Since each domain examines different aspects of the observable world, and each has its own analytical and theoretical traditions, the types of simulations and the approaches to using them will vary across subject areas. Simulations can provide experiences to support both content and process goals that make up domain knowledge.

The final consideration that "focuses upon the particular context where play/learning takes place, including macro-level historical, political and economic factors as well as micro-level factors such as the availability of specific resources and tools" (p. 253) will be addressed at the conclusion of the book.[22] While not central to the analysis of this project, there are some important considerations to make when thinking about the broader contexts and supports for the use of simulations. Chapter 5 will address many of these issues and will be a synthesis, pulling together the pedagogical, developmental, and cognitive and metacognitive considerations related to simulations.

Two

Learning Theories and Pedagogical Approaches to Simulations

> In my view, in the 21st century we need the following—and we need them fast and all at once together: embodied empathy for complex systems; "grit" (passion + persistence); playfulness that leads to innovation; design thinking; collaborations in which groups are smarter than the smartest person in the group; and real understanding that leads to problem solving and not just test passing. These are, to my mind, the true 21st century skills. We will not get them in schools alone and we will never get them in the schools we currently have.
>
> (p. 4)[6]

In the quote above, linguist and learning expert Gee does an effective job outlining not only the aims for schooling to support 21st century skills, but also a challenge to the *status quo* in schools today. He argued that digital games are uniquely positioned to support instructional practices that work toward achieving these goals. In this chapter, the general pedagogical considerations of digital simulations will be examined when applied to frameworks used to inform teaching. These considerations will provide a sense of how teaching practices using simulations can support various learning theories (e.g., constructivism, conceptual change theory) and instructional approaches (e.g., inquiry-based teaching).

We will address the learning framework and pedagogical considerations in a broad sense as related to simulations. Simulations can support the educator in making the phenomena being explored more approachable to the student and draw attention to key aspects therein; these supports can be critical when applying them within learning and instructional frameworks. As an example of these supports, teachers can use simulations to modify the speed and scale of phenomena to a level more appropriate to students' needs and interests. And because these phenomena can often be domain- and concept-specific, more detailed examples will be used to illustrate these applications.

ORGANIZATION OF THE CHAPTER

This chapter will be divided into two sections. The first half of the chapter will address how simulations support student thinking within research-supported learning frameworks. The focus here is on more constructivist models of teaching, as simulations have been most associated with supporting classroom practices that address authentic problem solving, teacher-facilitated inquiry, and empirical examinations of simulated phenomena. The second section is more practical, focusing on actions teachers can take to facilitate this learning while using simulations. When thinking of this kind of constructivist learning, we must consider pedagogical approaches like using learning progressions to be a guide in creating appropriate simulation experiences. With these approaches in mind, teachers and administrators can better understand how simulations may work in their classrooms and which of these simulations will meet the

Learning Theories and Pedagogical Approaches   29

needs of their students. Using existing learning frameworks, this chapter will outline how this technology can be used to support our current understandings about how students learn.

LEARNING FRAMEWORKS AND SIMULATIONS

Generally speaking, studies have indicated that there are positive effects on student learning when using simulations in classrooms. The degree and nature of these effects, as you might expect, vary by simulation and instructional approach. While this research demonstrates the promise of simulations as learning tools, it is important to put their use in the context of the frameworks of effective learning theories. This section shows first what some of the key tenets of effective learning frameworks are and then delineates how simulations can support these tenets. Considering on which frameworks to focus, Gibson posed an important question related to primary learning outcomes or purposes when using simulations:

> whether simulations are useful tools for learning complex concepts and values or whether their primary purpose is in the teaching and learning of merely surface procedures and tasks. In their substantial overview of the research, De Jong and Van Joolingen make the distinction between simulations that contain "*conceptual* models" and those that are based on "*operational* models."
>
> (p. 117)[23]

This issue is key when thinking about learning frameworks and their relationship to simulations; the result is what drives the learning focus. If the focus is on operations, a more information-processing framework would be more appropriate; however, when learning conceptual models, more constructivist frameworks are suitable. No doubt, students can learn about procedures using simulations; however, simulations' strengths are most leveraged when students learn concepts through following these procedures and operations. For purposes here, the focus will be on goals related to conceptual learning, as students tend to learn procedures within a conceptual learning framework.

One of the core thinkers on learning theory that supports this more conceptual approach, Vygotsky, provided a learning framework.[24] Through his framework of social/cultural constructivism, support for learning, from the teacher and peers, is critical for understanding. Maximum student learning occurs in the zone of proximal development. In this type of learning experience, the development of skills and concepts happens when a student encounters a task that can be accomplished with support, or scaffolding, from a person with more expertise. Tasks below this zone are those that the learner can accomplish without help, while tasks above the zone are too difficult for students to complete, even with support. This scaffolding can include simplifying steps to a process, asking thought-provoking questions, drawing attention to critical aspects of the experience, encouraging working with peers, and facilitating reflection and thinking aloud. This support, through teachers or more knowledgeable peers, is a necessary component in this learning framework.

Learning Theories and Pedagogical Approaches 31

Another constructivist learning theorist, Piaget, emphasized the notion of schema and cognition.[25] Schema provide cognitive structures that allow students to make sense of new information. Through a process that uses these schema, students assimilate, adapt, and balance in order then to incorporate, modify, and replace their existing ideas as they experience new phenomena. As students develop, they move from understanding based upon motor and sensory experiences to more abstract and indirect ways of knowing. The implication based on this theory is that children interact and learn from phenomena in different ways as they grow, which is important to keep in mind when working with simulations: the simulated experience for 5-year-old will likely be vastly different from that of a 15-year-old. Therefore, these simulations must be designed and supported by instructors in different ways to be matched to age groups and developmental levels.

When looking at these learning frameworks that foster conceptual understanding, a broad research consensus has emerged over the past few decades. In the National Research Council's book *How Students Learn*, they outlined key elements that support student learning in history, mathematics, and science.[26] These include the notion that students bring ideas about concepts, that learning information requires a connection to a broader conceptual framework, and that metacognition is important.[27] For an example of an instructional approach supported by the findings of *How Students Learn*, conceptual change theory in science education requires an understanding of the student's conceptual ecology, an attention to an idea's status, and the learner being able to discuss how they are processing this information.[28] The student's conceptual ecology includes the ideas they bring when examining a topic and the relationships these ideas have between other concepts in their mind. The status of an idea depends on how well the student understands a concept, whether it is useful to them, and whether the concept is believable. When they encounter a new phenomenon that they are trying to understand, they can see if it fits into an existing framework (i.e. assimilation). However, if this framework fails to adequately explain this new experience, the student becomes dissatisfied and may choose to modify that framework (i.e. accommodation) to better meet the student's needs. Drawing on Elby and Hammer's work on epistemological framing is useful to help understand how student ideas are resources children productively use when learning about scientific phenomena.[29] As the teacher identifies these ideas, they can help guide the student toward more sophisticated ways of knowing.

Simulations and games provide promising vehicles for this kind of learning. While simulations can offer an environment in which a constructivist model of learning can be supported, the educator must either design or intervene to create an experience to support students in this conceptual change process. For example, a student might believe that objects with more mass fall at a faster rate than those with less mass. To understand where this idea comes from, the teacher can ask how they justify this explanation, perhaps by asking what are the experiences or observations that lead to this conclusion? From this prompting, students may reference a common experience of observing a feather falling slower than another heavier object—a pencil or a book. Using this information, the teacher can provide a simulated experience that might allow the student to explore related phenomena in different contexts. For example, a teacher might lead the class using a simulation that demonstrates dropping a feather and a marble in a vacuum to show that they fall at the same rate. This experience is designed to provide students an opportunity to reconsider their ideas in the new context or add sophistication to their current explanation. A key part of this process is an attention to metacognition: an open discussion of students' ideas and their development. Teacher prompts, either written or verbal, help facilitate this discussion.

In the example above, gravity and air resistance are phenomena with which students have first-hand experience. However, when developing conceptual understanding, students often have a difficult time grasping those concepts with which they have little personal experience in real-life (e.g., electromagnetism, impressionism, demand-side economics). In a most basic sense, simulations can make the intangible more tangible, while also being engaging for students. While discussing learning physical science concepts when using game-based simulations, Squire et al. stated:

> Experiences in game worlds become experiences that students can draw upon in thinking about scientific worlds, using their intuitive understandings developed in simulated worlds to interpret physics problems. By representing complex scientific content through tangible,

experienced non-textually mediated representations, simulated worlds may also engage reluctant learners in the study of science.

(p. 513)[9]

In writing about learning and games, Gee discussed the importance of these experiences in learning. These experiences can be drawn upon to help inform encounters with new phenomena to develop their own learning:

> People store these experiences in memory—and human long-term memory is now viewed as nearly limitless—and use them to run simulations in their minds to prepare for problem solving in new situations. These simulations help them to form hypotheses about how to proceed in the new situation based on past experiences.
>
> (p. 21)[30]

He also later described the conditions simulations support through the development of student learning. These included experiences that are 1) structured by goals, 2) interpreted to understand what was learned and how that might inform future action, 3) examined to be given feedback, 4) used to apply in new situations, and 5) shared and interpreted with other people. These conditions for learning through experience can be applied to simulations. By their nature, simulations allow learning for deep understanding because they tend to push students to be more active in the instructional process. However, the simulation does not function in a vacuum. Critical in this process includes a curricular design or instructional approach that includes goals, space for students to interpret their experiences, peer and student feedback, and opportunities to apply what they have learned to new situations.

This active approach to learning runs counter to models of learning that focus on procedural or fact-based outcomes; however, when aiming for learning with a focus on durable understanding, students must engage with the material in a way that allows them to actively connect new content with existing understandings and schema. What we also know about learning is that information needs to be contextualized in the instructional environment. What simulations can provide are learning opportunities that are "situated and tacit," as opposed to decontextualized and explicit in more passive, direct-instructional frameworks. When examining the applications of augmented reality simulations, Dunleavy, Dede, and Mitchell stated:

> Contrary to conventional K-12 instruction, where knowledge is decontextualized and explicit, in [augmented reality] the learning is situated and tacit. This parallels the nature of 21st century work, in which problem finding (the front-end of the inquiry process: making observations and inferences, developing hypotheses, and conducting experiments to test alternative interpretations of the situation) is crucial to reaching a point where the work team can do problem solving. Workers' individual and collective meta-cognitive strategies for making meaning out of complexity (such as making judgments about the value of alternative problem formulations) are vital.
>
> (pg. 19)[10]

In addition to augmented reality simulations, game-based simulations can also provide a context-rich, student-driven leaning experience, as Gee noted: "Good games give information 'on demand' and 'just in time,' not out of the contexts of actual use or apart from people's purposes and goals, something that happens too often in schools" (p. 2).[31]

As noted by learning theorists, the social context is also an important component to developing understanding. Educational games and simulations can provide communities of practice to aid in this social leaning.[32] These important learning networks can be supported through games:

> Participatory cultures emerge around affinity spaces where people of different ability levels share information and skills and solve emergent problems. Participatory cultures describe how environments, such as video games, generate a wide range of indicators of engagement.
> (p. 388)[15]

To help support a variety of students, Gee observed the variability in the social experience of students within the gaming environment:

> Even single-player gaming often involves young people in joint play, collaboration, competition, sharing, and a myriad of websites, chat rooms, and game guides, many of them produced by players themselves. But the social nature of gaming goes much further. Multiplayer gaming (i.e. games where small teams play against each other) is very popular among many young people. And massively

multiplayer games (i.e. games where thousands or millions of people play the same game) have recently (thanks, in part, to the tremendous success of *World of WarCraft*) become mainstream forms of social interaction across the globe. Such games are introducing new "states" (six million people worldwide for *World of WarCraft*) or "communities" into the world.

(p. 197)[2]

The variability in platform and functionality within educational games and simulations allows the instructor to tailor the learning experience to meet the specific needs of a variety of audiences.

The use of simulations can foster the key components incorporated within innovative learning frameworks including constructivism and conceptual change theory. However, for simulations to be used effectively to these ends, teachers need to encourage students to examine their existing ideas, connect facts to existing domain-specific theoretical frameworks (game theory, Newtonian physics, macroeconomics), and engage in metacognitive strategies (reflection). In the next sections, we will explore methods to support these activities.

How Simulations Can Support Finding and Judging Existing Conceptions

To gather information about ideas that students have about a concept, the teacher can use a pre-simulation quiz; another method is to use the simulation with prompts to examine their current ideas. For example, in an economics simulation, students may observe that raising the price of soup causes a large decrease in sales; however, the same doesn't happen with the price increase of a candy bar. The teacher can then ask students to use their existing understanding of the concept of supply and demand to try to explain the data they see. The discrepancy in market reactions may allow students an opportunity to examine and consider the usefulness of their existing ideas and epistemological framing to lead to greater sophistication of their explanatory models—perhaps by adding notions of elasticity and inelasticity into their models. Simulations can trigger thinking through real-world video snippets, simulated examples, and data to be examined. To facilitate this, students need to be encouraged by the teacher to bring their ideas and connect them to new experiences.

When students are more aware of their ideas, the simulated experiences provide them with opportunities to examine their existing explanations of phenomena. Unexpected results can help motivate students in this examination, as they can lead to questions about their current explanatory models. For example, in the *MEteor* simulation, students may explore the idea that after a force acts on an object in space, the effect dissipates—that is, the object will slow down, even with no other forces acting upon it. During the simulation where the task is to hit a target with a meteor, students may launch a meteor with too much velocitywith the assumption that the velocity will decrease as the object travels. Feedback from the simulation shows that this is not the case leading students to reconsider their existing idea to successfully accomplish the task.[7]

How Simulations Can Support Connecting Facts to Domain-Specific Frameworks

Teachers can support putting observations into a set of broader frameworks by requiring students to situate experiences with simulated phenomena into a larger conceptual context. For example, if students observe the effects of crime in a simulated city, they can put the data into a broader socio-political context, depending on supports like the presence or absence of social safety nets. This practice helps students build connections between their experiences and domain-specific frameworks, which in turn can foster deeper learning.

To illustrate the connection between experience and domain-specific frameworks, Cantrell, Pekcan, Itani, and Velasquez-Bryant used simulations and hands-on prototype design with middle school students to work through engineering problems. Using the experiences from both the simulated and physical prototype building, they found that special education students showed dramatic learning gains in science concepts. They stated:

> The engaging nature of the engineering design project compelled students to interact with materials and ideas in a variety of learning activities that required them to gain a conceptual understanding of science ideas in order to successfully design and build their projects. By engaging in the engineering design process, students had no choice but to come to an understanding of these ideas if they hoped to build a successful project. Students were then able to apply their knowledge to mental problem solving as well as to hands-on problem solving. This alternative

approach to learning science would be particularly beneficial for students with learning disabilities.

(p. 307)[33]

In this approach, students were engaged in a problem and learned science concepts within an engineering framework. Additionally, the dichotomy of process and content was broken down. Students learned fact-based knowledge by working through a problem-solving process. Engineering design, meant to solve a particular problem, served as a framework to connect facts to each other.

One method to support student learning while connecting it to domain-specific frameworks is the use of familiar experiences. In this example, providing more support through movement can be helpful, as noted by Lindgren et al.:

> Using one's body within the simulation naturally allows students to enact a set of movements with which they are familiar from everyday life (walking, running, etc.). While the novelty of this simulation may certainly have some effect on students' self-reported enjoyment and learning, we argue that it is the familiarity of such movements as well as the higher degree of physical involvement that decreases the distance between knowledge that learners perceive to be difficult to learn, leading to the higher overall gains on an assessment of participant attitudes towards science.
>
> (p. 182)[7]

The authors noted that the movement allowed the students to "be there," making the abstract science concepts more concrete to the learners. In this case, movement, when facilitated through the simulation, provided a connection between the abstract simulated world and the more tangible experiences of students.

How Simulations Can Support Metacognition

Again, supporting metacognition and reflection is a place where the teacher has a major role. In experientially based learning opportunities, students must be provided supports and encouragement to reflect upon their experiences to apply what they have learned to new, relevant situations.[34] Using debriefing techniques, from the teacher and/or within the simulation, after a simulated experience can help students think about how they processed the information presented in the simulation. These techniques can include questions that ask students to justify their explanations, discuss which simulated phenomena informed their learning, assess their most current understandings, and formulate the next steps to help further develop their knowledge.

While opportunities for reflection can be part of the simulation, studies suggest that this reflection must be fostered by an explicit instruction. As Vos noted,

> [A]uthentic assessment is a concept built upon a number of principles of effective assessment, and one that is grounded in a 'real-world' learning situation reflects many features of the simulation game experience. At the very least, the literature on authentic assessment offers evidence-based principles upon which tutors can benchmark their assessment strategies. However, no matter how well designed the assessment is, other factors such as student characteristics and environmental factors can

> also affect the assessment structure and outcomes. An authentic learning experience or an authentic assessment will not create itself. The willingness of the student to engage with the simulation and their prior skills, and the role of the tutor in structuring the experience plus the assessment tasks is critical to participants gaining the maximum learning benefits.
>
> (p. 63)[35]

Students need support in how to think about their thinking in general, and the complexity of simulations often requires more instructional guidance to help draw their attention toward experiences that are most relevant to their learning. Using features that pause, isolate, or highlight aspects of the simulated phenomena can help students focus on aspects most relevant to their learning process.

Through applying constructivist learning frameworks, simulations can function to support critical student actions that facilitate understanding concepts. These actions include students examining their existing ideas, connecting facts to theoretical frameworks, and engaging in metacognitive strategies. While simulations can provide an environment to make these actions possible, the instructor must play a vital role to encourage these ways of learning. In the next section, we will explore some of the pedagogical approaches that best leverage simulations to support this learning.

PEDAGOGICAL APPROACHES

While it may be tempting to use simulations as a proxy for the instructor or to merely present students' information in a more interesting way, simulations do require

Learning Theories and Pedagogical Approaches 43

intervention on the teacher's part. This aspect presents a unique challenge for educators to teach in nontraditional ways to best utilize the strengths of simulations. As noted below by Lane and Peres, simulations require a pedagogical approach that facilitates deeper engagement with the simulated phenomena:

> The key point is that using simulations in a way that spoon feeds students by providing them with knowledge without requiring that they actively pursue that knowledge is relatively ineffective.
>
> (p. 3)[36]

The challenges teachers face using non-simulation-based instruction are not different from those faced when using this technology. Gee noted the importance of not merely viewing educational games as being engaging on their own:

> What makes video games good for learning is not, by any means, just the fact that they are games. Furthermore, the video games that are most interesting for learning are not just any video games. Different types of game[s] can have different effects. Puzzle games like *Tetris* and *Bejeweled* may very well exercise pattern recognition capacities; *Trivial Pursuit* games may well make learning facts fun. But these are not, in my view, the sorts of video games which are most interesting in regard to learning.
>
> (p. 198)[2]

When using simulations, if teachers fail to engage students in meaningful problems or scenarios, do not provide the necessary scaffolding of observation and analytical skills, or take a hands-off approach in design or implementation of instruction, students will not be particularly successful in meeting the intended leaning outcomes. Studies suggest that simulations, as stand-alone learning tools, will not necessarily improve student learning and do not serve as a replacement for good, teacher-facilitated instruction. In this sense, they will not replace the role of a teacher.

While the simulation equipment can be prohibitively expensive to buy, maintain, and update, this consideration is only a small portion of the fiscal cost of bringing simulations to the classroom. Professional development and support may present a much higher cost in both money and time. As with many new techniques and technologies applied to the classroom, ongoing professional development is critical in regards to simulations.[10] One-day workshops about these new applications is a start but not effective to insure their implementation. The need for ongoing support is important for instructional technology, but especially pressing for simulations.

When considering the praxis of learning frameworks and pedagogical approaches, game-based learning expert Squire described the importance of seeing educational games as **designed experiences**.[37] Often, instructional design incorporates inputs (instruction and curriculum) and outputs (assessment). Unfortunately, the processes of learning are treated as black boxes and are not closely examined or addressed in curriculum design. Applying a designed-experience approach to curriculum using simulations and educational games allows the learning experience to be treated less as a black box, bringing the

Learning Theories and Pedagogical Approaches 45

learning process out in the open. Being attentive to both the design of inputs—the simulation activities—and the outputs—how learning is assessed—is key to understanding how simulations can most effectively aid learning. An attention to how students build mental models can be a useful aspect of simulation activities to provide a better sense of how students develop understanding, as Gee observed in examining game-based simulations:

> Gamers are engaged in building a model of a model in order to play games. Let me give one simple example. In the animé game *Valkyria Chronicles*, players engage in what looks like warfare with tanks and all. When I played the game I first assumed that the game was, like many other games (e.g., *Call of Duty*), a model of real-world warfare. I carefully protected my soldiers behind cover and moved them up slowly and carefully, attempting to remove all opposing forces before moving to the final goal. None of this works well in the game (though it works well in *Call of Duty*). The fighting in *Valkyria Chronicles* is, in fact, a model of "capture the flag" in multiplayer games, not real-world warfare. You need to move fast past the opposition to get one soldier up to the goal. Playing this game requires players to see that the game is a simulation (model) of capture the flag and then work out (model) how that the simulation works so they can be successful in the game.
>
> (p. 5)[6]

This greater sense of how students are actively learning from the simulation can serve to support metacognitive outcomes. Gee believed that gaming simulations allowed students to use design-based thinking, which he defined as "thinking about how various parts of a system (e.g., different sub-systems within a system) or different systems interact with each other" (p. 6).[6] Supporting this part-whole destination and design-thinking, gamers are able to switch between a more situated perspective (more in the moment) with global perspectives (seeing the whole of the game).[6] Further supporting the design experience approach, game-based learning experts Halverson and Steinkuehler noted that games can enhance multiple key pedagogical actions that support learning frameworks as students work through game-based problems:

> The interaction required for successful game play draws the player in to learn the interface, to master what makes an appropriate move in the space, to learn from failure and to explore how to seek help. Each of these behaviors is a key feature of successful learning, and each is required in even the most humble game environments.
>
> (p. 376)[15]

While simulations and games will never replace good instruction, the nature of this technology will force a change in how teachers work. Collins and Halverson discussed some of the critical incompatibilities between traditional formal schooling and technology. These incompatibilities include the following scenarios:

- Uniform learning vs. Customization: Schooling often focuses on a singular approach to instruction. Technology allows for tremendous customization to address student interest and challenges.

- Teacher as expert vs. Diverse knowledge sources: Instead of the teacher being the font of knowledge in the classroom, technology can provide information from many sources.
- Standardized assessment vs. Specialization: New technologies can allow students the opportunity to choose their own paths to meeting objectives, making successful performances look different than traditional multiple choice objective exams.
- Knowledge in the head vs. Reliance on outside resources: Instead of equating internalized knowledge as a singular goal of learning, the ability to pull resources from multiple sources is a valuable skill when using technology.
- Coverage vs. The knowledge explosion: With the increase in both access to and amount of information available due to technology, it has become increasingly difficult to cover all topics (with depth) necessary in life.
- Learning by acquisition vs. Learning by doing: Technology allows for more inquiry- and activity-based pedagogy. These approaches contrast with the more traditional direct instruction teaching approaches. (p. 2–3)[1]

Each of these incompatibilities can be seen as a weakness for simulations, but if traditional pedagogical approaches can be modified or replaced, these incompatibilities can become strengths. Collins and Halverson make the case that these changes in approach are imperatives in using technology like simulations:

> We encapsulate those imperatives in terms of *customization, interaction, and control*. Customization refers to providing

> people the knowledge they want when they want it and to supporting and guiding them as they learn. Interaction refers to the ability of computers to give learners immediate feedback and to engage learners through simulation in accomplishing realistic tasks. Control refers to putting learners in charge of their learning, so they feel ownership and can direct their learning where their interests take them.
>
> (p. 8)[1]

While some of the more direct instructional methods, including providing practice-and-drill exercises, are found within a simulated experience (practicing landing a plane using set procedures), they are often not the primary focus of these simulations. Game-based simulations that are connected to academic concepts are uniquely positioned to support development of more conceptual understanding than lower-order objectives (facts, rules, procedures):

> I argue that games are a good model for designing such experiences because they are interactive systems, not content dissemination devices. Learning through games (and other simulated systems)—whether digital or analog—is not a process of information presentation, reception absorption and repetition, but interactive meaning making and construction.
>
> (p. 304)[38]

A paradox emerges when considering the effective use of simulations: While teacher involvement in curriculum and design is necessary for their success, fully leveraging their use tends to lend itself toward more indirect approaches

Learning Theories and Pedagogical Approaches 49

to instruction. This conundrum comes into play when focusing on higher-order outcomes, which increases the importance of curriculum design and intentionality during the limited teacher-led moments during simulation activities. One key pedagogical orientation is that the teacher has an important role in working with simulations. In their review of the literature surrounding the use of simulations in science education, Smetana and Bell observed that "there has been consensus about the use of computer simulations as a supplement to, rather than a substitute for, other learning activities" (p. 1352).[20]

Simulations can provide interactive laboratories to allow students to do more **inductive reasoning**. In this kind of thinking, students find a pattern in the data and develop an explanation for it. For example, a math student might examine a graph of data showing the relationship between pressure and volume by calculating the slope of a line. Simulations allow students the opportunity to "run" an investigation quickly, generating data immediately from multiple trials. Large amounts of data can be created and presented in multiple formats (line graphs, raw numbers) that allow the teachers to scaffold students appropriately. With this presentation of data with the appropriate amount of clarity, students can then observe patterns and develop explanatory models based on those patterns they see.

Simulations can also help the instructor control what should be the center of the student's focus, which is valuable in the learning process, as noted by Fraser et al.:

> Learning is enhanced when a critical aspect of a phenomenon is varied while all other aspects are kept constant.

> The implication of this is that any simulation should allow for variation of a critical aspect of a phenomenon, while keeping other aspects constant (invariant).
>
> (p. 382)[14]

A teacher can eliminate distractors, simplify the objects under consideration, and draw attention to more pertinent aspects of the simulation. For example, when examining a simulation about the Earth's population through time, it is conceivable that such a simulation could include data related to age, gender, ethnographic distributions, and geographic spread of populations. To illustrate the effect of war on populations, the teacher may ask students to focus exclusively on age and gender when they run the simulation. The important implication here is that the instructor serves an important role when using simulations.

In considering the most effective pedagogical approaches when using simulations, the emerging research suggests that a guided discovery methodology provides for the most appropriate and impactful use of simulations. Relatedly, simulations are most effective when they (a) are used as supplements (b) incorporate high-quality support structures (c) encourage student reflection; and (d) promote cognitive dissonance.[20] Smetana and Bell noted the importance of teacher involvement to best support the use of these simulations:

> Furthermore, allowing the flexibility to explore ideas, as well as prompting students to justify their actions and providing timely feedback, are additional factors that may have promoted learning with simulations. However, there

is evidence that students may not take full advantage of these features or opportunities if not given the time, support, or encouragement to do so. Similarly, the importance of the teacher in providing guidance and support during simulation use is clearly demonstrated.

(p 1356)[20]

The research suggests that designing curriculum to provide additional instructional support will result in greater learning gains when compared to just using the simulations on their own. Smetana and Bell went on to describe the nature of these instructional supports:

Support structures may include providing time for familiarization with the simulation, teacher direction, questioning, debriefing of learning activities, feedback about decisions and actions, opportunity for reflection, accompanying assignments, and access to other tools and domain knowledge.

(p. 1358)[20]

These instructional supports might include the teacher helping students articulate their observations of phenomena, noting what learning to reflect upon, and questioning student conclusions.

Simulations are shown to be most effective when they supplement instruction, utilize support structures, foster student reflection, and challenge students' existing ideas.[20] From a curriculum design standpoint, simulations do not pose a wildly different instructional challenge from other more traditional learning tools. Effective instruction often includes clear goals, opportunities for students to explore phenomena, ample feedback, and support for struggling students. For example, Frederking, while working with college students studying political science, synthesized his curriculum design of simulation activities to include the following: a) instructional objectives, b) design of the simulation, c) simulation preparation with the students, d) the simulation activity itself, and d) a debrief activity.[13]

An educator may choose a simulation because it provides a learning opportunity that is more flexible, safe, and efficient than the actual experience.[20] These goals can be achieved through the use of animations and visualizations that provide more idealized realities. The phenomena under examination may be difficult to see or discern what is important to observe. Additionally, these simulations can affect the scale of phenomena to help students see them more clearly. For example, a simulation may speed up a time scale to make a process more discernible—the evolution of a society is much easier, and more feasible, considering the limitations of a class period, to grasp in minutes rather than decades, or even centuries. As another example, a phenomenon that is too large or too small—cell division, perhaps—to see in person can be brought to a more manageable size scale.

One of the first instructional considerations is determining the objectives or goals for the simulation activity. Addressing this question centers on how to orient students to the relevant task. The novelty of the application may present some pedagogical difficulty with the students. It has been reported that students have been

Learning Theories and Pedagogical Approaches

so engaged with the virtual world using augmented reality that they pay little attention to their actual surrounding space.[10] This particular behavior presents a safety issue, but also creates a disconnect between the reality and the augmentation, making it difficult for students to develop a true understanding of phenomena. Additionally, students may be more interested in the functionality of the application than to the content of this functionality.[10] For example, students might be excited to be able to communicate with each other virtually, while paying little attention to what they are communicating about, not only serving as a distraction to learning, but also as a waste of valuable class time.

While immersive simulations like augmented reality provide some challenges, whole-body experiences may do more to aid students' learning. Lindgren et al. noted how learning was better facilitated when using a whole-body simulation experience:

> Only in the whole-body condition, however, did the participants make their predictions and enact their understanding through gross body movement embedded within the simulation, entailing a first-person rather than—as in the desktop condition—a birds-eye perspective on a scientific phenomenon. The learner becomes an active partner in creating and experiencing science events that frequently challenge their expectations and counter their intuitions. Rather than relying on physical interaction alone, from within the *MEteor* simulation participants can merge their sensorimotor perceptions with augmented representations and digital scaffolds that make critical concepts salient.
>
> (p. 182)[7]

As compared to the desktop version of the simulation, the immersive nature of the whole-body simulation allowed students a deeper perspective on the phenomena being explored.

In their work with the *MEteor* application, used to teach students about object trajectory in space, Lindgren et al. stated that students showed a greater understanding of physics and had a more positive affect toward the experience when they used a whole-body simulation versus the desktop computer version.[7] As noted earlier, the concrete nature of using a motion-capture device allowed students more of an opportunity to interact with the phenomena. Additionally, the immersive floor and wall projections of information allowed students to become more of a part of the simulation experience.

Creating another pedagogical issue is the quality of many simulations to be quite sophisticated, providing many avenues of exploration and study. Narrowing the scope of the required tasks would help manage the cognitive load for students, and some simulations provide the flexibility for teachers to have more input. For example, the design principles of the *Alien Contact!* program state these objectives:

> (1) build in multiple entry points for teachers, (2) build in mathematical and linguistic patterns that, when recognized, reveal the ubiquity and mystery of mathematics and language, and (3) build in multiple layers of complexity that will engage and challenge students regardless of ability and will provide teachers opportunities for differentiation.
>
> (p. 11)[10]

Using this kind of application, teachers can modify the topic, decide how much interaction they will have with the students, and direct how students work with the simulation. In an example of how simulation designers built in attention to student need, Wang, Wu, and Hsu created a physics simulation that displayed important and relevant information on the computer screen instead of requiring students to remember it.[8] In this design, they were attentive to students' cognitive load as well as their active engagement.

Another model to manage their cognitive load and scaffold students' learning is what science education researcher Adams called "engaged exploration," where students work with the simulation in a way similar to how a scientist might approach a problem. This approach "involves students actively thinking, sense-making, and exploring via their own questioning" (p. 9).[19] In studying college students working with the *PhET* simulations for math and science, she found that supports within the simulation that included tapping into a student's prior understanding, clues when working through a problem, and self-pacing were more successful developing a conceptual understanding the physics content (circuits, electromagnetism, waves).[19] Adams described this "engaged exploration" process:

> The simulations have implicit guidance and balanced challenges which encourage engaged exploration where students approach problem solving and knowledge acquisition in a similar fashion as experts. Engaged exploration with simulations in the no guidance or open conceptual question condition provides only enough guidance

> to require students to explore via their own questioning. Students form a mental framework through this process. Through its design (controls, features, visualizations), the simulation can influence this framework, shaping it into one that is similar to an expert's.
>
> (p. 10)

This deeper conceptual understanding was developed even though these students were provided limited guidance within the simulation and by the teacher about the functions and sequencing of the simulation.

When using simulations as a supplement to non-digital instruction, the Teachers Integrating Engineering into Science (TIES) program was designed to support engineering practice with middle school students.[33] In this program, a blended model of instruction was used to help students develop an understanding of science content related to force through an engineering design process where students worked with the simulation to generate, examine, and reflect upon data. Then, using the data from the simulation, students designed a physical prototype to solve an engineering problem. Three problem modules were used; they included the designs of a hot-air balloon, car bumpers, and bridges. The process was iterative, with students learning about phenomena, and testing ideas with the simulation through the creation of physical testing prototypes. Student learning supports included science content information within the simulation and feedback and discussion with peer groups working on the same engineering problem. Results showed decreases in achievement gaps across some demographic groups on standardized achievement tests.

When considering supports for student simulation use, the instructor must decide how much to teach students about the function of the simulation itself. Can students work through and understand the simulation on their own, or is it complicated enough to require explicit instruction about the application? How much time is appropriate to dedicate to the purpose? As an example of student support would include creating a worksheet to guide students while working with simulation activities. In their study examining the use of simulations in college engineering coursework, Fraser et al. provided students a worksheet that focused on drawing a conceptual understanding versus using the simulation only to make the required calculations in the activity. They found that students were already able to approach the phenomena in a quantitative manner when using the simulation only, but they showed little understanding of the concepts.[14]

In the activity, students were asked to record qualitative descriptions, as opposed to strictly using computational representations based on the qualitative data. Students demonstrated a more sophisticated conceptual understanding after using the worksheets while studying the simulated phenomena. However, Fraser et al. reported that college engineering students did not find simulation activities as a way to learn material. They concluded that simulations must be used earlier in the instructional process, when students are still relatively unfamiliar with the content.

In addition to some of the more domain-specific outcomes, other skills like teamwork and collaboration can be fostered to help support students working with simulations. Simulation tasks can be structured in such a way as to require students to work together in teams. Tasks can be divided so that students need to use jigsaw techniques to bring their unique perspectives to the team to solve a problem; as such, each team member would be required to bring specific and unique information to a problem when all students participate.[10] These pedagogical techniques can foster "communities of practice," which can then become important components of the social nature of learning supported by Vygotsky. These supports provide another example of the important role of the instructor, who would need to foster the development of these skills.

When considering assessment and reflection upon learning, assessment must support a more contextualized view of student understanding. **Authentic assessment**, a form of assessment meant to mirror real-world tasks, can support this view of student understanding. In Vos' review of design frameworks and authentic assessment for use with simulations, she described eight key areas of consensus:

1. The real-world value of the assessment task;
2. Students perform or create a product as the output;
3. Challenge and complexity of tasks and issues of transfer;
4. Known criteria and assessment literacy;
5. Developmental opportunities with formative assessment and regular feedback;

6. Sufficient and varied activities to make up the whole;
7. Opportunities for reflection; and
8. Interaction and collaboration. (p. 59)[35]

Simulations are uniquely positioned to address each of these areas, as they tend to be designed in a manner that allows students to demonstrate their understanding within a (simulated) real-world and dynamic context.[35] Students are able to show their understanding through various levels of performances through the simulation, which can be demonstrated quickly as success or failure within the simulated environment. Using the simulation, the assessment can become part of the learning process by providing immediate feedback through the system. Additionally, while working within constructivist frameworks, simulations can provide scaffolding through online feedback and support from learning communities (from peers or experts) as students progress toward deeper understanding.

While not a central focus of this book, some studies have found positive effects when using digital simulations with students with disabilities with engagement and with the flexibility of technology to meet the needs of students. **Universal Design** is one promising direction to make simulations more accessible to all students. Key elements of Universal Design include understanding the goals for the simulation, the barriers to learning using this technology, the ways to overcome these barriers, and a mechanism to evaluate the accessibility of the simulation.[39] Determining what learning outcomes are most central to the lesson is a first step. This can be useful in eliminating distractions and focusing students on the most relevant aspects of the simulation. Making sure students can provide input with a mouse, touchscreen, or motion sensors is a critical consideration when determining the barriers to working with the simulation. Managing the amount and types of images, text, sounds, and animations might be important when examining the kinds of outputs the simulation provides students. Finally, the instructor should collect data as to the successes and challenges students face when working with the technology.

Equity is another issue that teachers face when working with simulations. Bring Your Own Device may be an option to decrease both the cost to schools and also the leaning time required to understand and use the technology. However, access to the devices and networking capabilities may be highly variable because of financial barriers. Collins and Halverson also brought up several key equity issues as technology advances into educational settings, and these settings continue to evolve:

> ***Equity.*** Despite widespread tracking and segregation, the public schools are the institution that fosters equity more than any other institution. If education fractionates and the states relinquish responsibility for giving students an education, then poor children are likely to suffer.
>
> ***Citizenship and Social cohesion.*** In Jefferson's and Horace Mann's vision, education would prepare people to be good citizens and assimilate them to a common culture. Mann was very concerned about educating immigrants and developing social cohesion. In such fractionation by interest

Learning Theories and Pedagogical Approaches 61

groups, citizenship and social cohesion goals may be undermined.

Diversity. As education fractionates, people may learn less about people from other backgrounds and cultures. Hence, we may find it difficult to get along with people from different backgrounds or with different views.

Broader horizons. When people select their own education goals, they pick things that interest them or that are occupation-oriented. Their choices are often narrowly focused. But a major goal of education is to expand people's horizons. (p. 7)[1]

Future design of simulations will need to address these issues with equity in mind. Miller and Kocurek noted some of the parameters to address as educational games often have been limited in the treatment of women and minorities:

> Given such disparities between gender on a variety of media platforms, we urge developers to consider the gender roles such as gender balance and other demographic variables including occupation, age, and income status of their characters in games.
>
> (p. 323)[21]

KEY TAKEAWAYS FROM THIS CHAPTER

Simulations provide unique supports for learning frameworks (conceptual change theory) and teaching approaches (inquiry-based instruction). Tasks can be structured to both identify and provide opportunities for students to explore their ideas about concepts and allow them to reflect upon their thinking. Using these frameworks the educator must be able to make the phenomena under study more appreciable to the student to draw attention to key aspects of the phenomena being explored. Many simulations can change the speed and scale of the elements contained within to make the phenomena more accessible to students. As might not be surprising to the reader, good general pedagogical techniques and guidelines apply equally well to simulations as they do to other aspects of teaching.

Teacher support and scaffolding may be necessary to enhance student outcomes using these applications. Structuring the simulation experience in a manner that allows students to be challenged, without overwhelming them, is a strength of those applications that offer the teacher the flexibility in deciding how they will be used in the classroom. The important takeaway is that there is a variance in the nature of user interaction with simulations. Understanding these differences better tailors the pedagogical experience for the best match to student learning and interests and to instructional goals. Chapter 3 will describe how these learning frameworks and pedagogical practices address different developmental contexts of students working with simulations

Three
Developmental Considerations of Simulations

> In Ms. Johnson's fourth grade class, students are learning about cell structures using touchscreen-enabled tablets. She chose to use a tablet because students were familiar and comfortable using the technology. Students, working in pairs, are using the tablets to "tour" animal cells. When students encounter a new cell structure, a dialog box appears that describes the function of that structure. Ms. Johnson has been attentive to each student's reading level and has modified these descriptions to better match student ability. While students are free to examine cell parts as they choose, the application periodically prompts students to make observations and reflect upon what they have learned.

In the vignette above, the teacher has made multiple instructional decisions based on her students' developmental level when using the cell simulation. Students' abilities physically and cognitively work with this tablet-based simulation where important considerations when working with the technology.

Chapter 3 will consider the benefits and uses of simulations for learners along the development spectrum. For example, how would using simulations in math or science differ with 8-year-old students versus 16-year-old students? This chapter provides a connection between the pedagogical considerations of Chapter 2 and the considerations of a student's development. For example, when examining learning, we should also consider pedagogical approaches like using learning progressions, or the sequence of skills that students complete to develop mastery, as guides when creating appropriate simulation experiences. What is important to understand is that instructional approaches must be modified when using technology that is developmentally appropriate for children.

The findings used in this chapter will encompass both types of technology used by games-based simulations and digital educational games. The inclusion of the full spectrum of these applications is appropriate here, as many of the issues associated with digital games are similarly applicable to simulations. For example, how younger students address cognitive multitasking or how they approach some of the physical challenges of larger handheld devices can apply to similar challenges found when using simulations. Broadening the findings to include educational games allows for a more comprehensive treatment of the developmental issues associated with using digital technology.

Of course, the above statement is made with a caveat: We must be cautious in making generalizations about students that are too broad, as individuals within generations vary, students within age cohorts vary, and developmental needs vary. To put it more bluntly, we need to understand both the individual technology and the individual student to find a match to design the most effective simulation-based learning experience, as noted by Athreya and Mouza:

Developmental Considerations of Simulations 65

> it is important to identify strategies for using new media practices to engage young audiences in productive uses of technology that benefit their thinking, learning, and overall well-being. When considering strategies for using technology, it is important to avoid polarized perspectives or "black and white" views. There are many articles that blame technology for a variety of problems, from the lack of reading or social skills to dangerous behaviors and addiction. But such concerns are not new. Almost every generation has feared that the next is too preoccupied with the latest technology, whether that is radio or television. Before decrying the detrimental effects of technology, it's worth considering the type of tasks young people engage in when using digital tools. In other words, we need to consider how "screen time" is used.
>
> (p. 22)[40]

Understanding how children currently interact with technology is important to best design the learning experience.

Key considerations would be similar to those used with any instructional tool. For instance, simulations can be selected based upon an attention to grade level and developmental level; accordingly, critical considerations include the nature of the representations, the supports provided by both the teacher and the simulation, the physical interaction between the simulation and the student, and the appropriateness of the subject matter.

Since many simulations offer a sort of simplified version of the real-world phenomena under consideration, attention must be given to the complexity of the representations and the nature of the learners. For example, text-heavy descriptions of the components of a representation may not be appropriate for early childhood students. Likewise, students who are struggling in math may have a challenging time with models that rely on algebraic reasoning as part of their explanation.

The supports provided by the teacher and simulation are important considerations when working with simulations as well. Students having a tough time grasping strategic processing may need scaffolding to ensure they are guided in doing more open-ended activities, like virtual laboratories. For these students, step-by-step simulations may be more appropriate.

How a student will work with the simulation is also a key developmental consideration when using the technology. Inputs that require too many keyboarding skills may not be appropriate for younger children, so opting for other options like touch screens and voice commands may be an appropriate and useful method that would allow these students access to the simulations.

Finally, subject matter must be considered. Thinking about the underlying real-world phenomena being represented is important when working toward developing a deep understanding of the subject matter. While a representation itself might be graspable, if students cannot connect it to the actual underlying concept, the learning becomes trivial. For example, students may be able to use virtual squares to make predictions about heredity, but if they do not understand the underlying concepts of Mendelian genetics, they will not truly understand the representation.

TECHNOLOGY PRACTICES OF CHILDREN

One challenge for educators when addressing the developmental needs of students when using technology in learning settings is that the digital experience is constantly evolving and expanding. Children born in the 1990s versus those born in the 2000s and 2010s have been raised with differing access to personal computers, networks, and mobile devices. The increase in use of smartphones and tablets in the 2000s and the ubiquity of wireless networks have meant the setting and use of digital devices and media have expanded into realms once reserved for traditional media and modes of communication. Students may now be reading authored texts on a tablet instead of in magazines and newspapers, ordering food using a smartphone instead of a tethered landline or at a food counter, streaming music instead of buying a compact disc, and using an e-ticket instead of a printed boarding pass to board a plane. Educators with the perspective of not having been raised with this technology may need an updated sense of the developmental needs of their students.

For early adolescents, much like younger children, it is important not only to think about the simulation itself but also the conceptual space in which students will work with the phenomena. Cell phones are a ubiquitous part of the lives of tweens and teens, used for more than just making phone calls.[40] That being said, the television still is a major source of media content, although the content is consumed differently now than it had been in the past. On demand, streaming, and digital recording has made television viewing asynchronous with network scheduling.[40] This may indicate

68 Developmental Considerations of Simulations

that students use many sources of content, but they do so on their own terms, meaning that children have a lot of power to choose which media they choose to use and how long they engage with it.

While students are getting more and more tech savvy, and at earlier and earlier ages, there are still important aspects to consider for younger children when using simulations in formal educational settings. Children of this age likely have limited awareness of the Internet, its risks, and its benefits, although they may use it regularly. Key trends with younger children include the following:

- Children learn from observing other family members including older siblings.
- Tablets are the device of choice.[41]

The Cooney Center examined the media habits of early-aged children and how these practices related to educational experiences.[42] Surprisingly, they found that children viewed more educational television than educational content on other digital media, such as tablets or computers. Another interesting finding related to children's use of digital media and how the purpose of this use evolved as they got older. While children spend more time with digital media as they age, their proportionate use of educational technology decreases. Simply having access to electronic reading devices did not necessarily result in follow-through; only half of them read on them.[40]

While the use of digital technology may be increasing, it is important to be cautious about assuming that all students interact with technology in the same way. There may be socioeconomic factors, disability considerations,

Developmental Considerations of Simulations

and parent and student choices (e.g., limiting "screen time") that affect access to digital technologies. Athreya and Mouza observed the diversity within what is often referred to as the "digital generation":

> Rather than assuming universal skill and knowledge with technology, we recognize that variations exist depending on a number of factors. These factors could include the social environment, gender, ethnic, and socio-economic status, as well as interest in and beliefs towards technology.
>
> (p. 13)[40]

The Pew Research Center found that the socioeconomic status of these teens' families affected their access to technology.[43] Differences in socioeconomic status also correlated with differences in the type of technology that was used at home. Teens from higher-income households, where parents have higher levels of education, were more likely to have desktop and laptop computers. These teens were among the most likely to own smartphones. In contrast, teens from lower-income households were most likely to have a basic cell phone. Teens from lower-income households were also less likely to have a game console (67% compared to 83% of teens in higher-income households). Additionally, teens from higher-income families went online more frequently compared to teens from lower income families.[40]

It is also important to keep in mind, when selecting appropriate simulations, that not all students develop at the same rate. Even within age cohorts, variance in physical factors such as hand size and vision acuity may present challenges for some students. While it might be easy to make assumptions about students in similar age groups, an understanding of their physical strengths and limitations should influence lesson design using simulations. When selecting hardware, the size of the hand-held devices and the types of input required (e.g., mouse, touchscreens) can be critical in determining students' likely success and comfort working with the simulation. For example, when using an augmented reality simulation, asking a smaller student to hold an iPad with one hand and providing a command via touchscreen with the other might be too difficult for younger children; in this case, hardware with a screen that doesn't have to be held—a desktop or a laptop, perhaps—may be a better option.

Beyond some of these more physical developmental factors, there are cognitive considerations to make as well. Bodemer, Ploetzne, Feuerlein, and Spada noted that while learning with simulations may be an advantage for some students, it might be a cognitive challenge for other learners:

> Frequently, it is taken for granted that the use of dynamic visualisations in computer-based learning environments is beneficial to learning. However, dynamic visualisations not only offer varied potential to learners but also place specific requirements on learners. These requirements are related to the dynamics and the interactivity of the visualisations, as well as to the features of the learning environment the visualisations are embedded in.
>
> (p. 326)[18]

The younger generations may have greater access to digital technology; however, this access can vary and

Developmental Considerations of Simulations 71

may not always be beneficial. These findings appear to counter the assumption that children can easily access educational content on devices like computers and tablets, choose to do so, and work with this technology in an educationally productive way. Understanding these trends helps educators understand children's digital media use and how to support that use for instructional purposes. For example, the heavy consumption of educational material from the television, a more passive technology, may poorly prepare children to use more active simulation interfaces such as those using touchscreens. Additionally, the notion of children passively receiving information from a television is quite different from the more active role required of them when processing information using a simulation. Preparing and supporting them for this more active role may be a vital concept for the educator to consider when designing educational experiences using simulations.

To address these challenges for the educator, key developmental considerations when using this technology in learning settings will be discussed in the next section.

HOW ARE THE DEVELOPMENTAL CONSIDERATIONS RELATED TO SIMULATIONS?

Being attentive to developmental challenges are important in aiding learning during simulation experiences. Miller and Kocurek outlined some of the critical developmental considerations in educational game design:

> Educational games should be developmentally appropriate—meaning that games should consider all developmental aspects of the targeted age including the physical,

motor, social, cognitive, and emotional domains. Understanding the developmental landscape at targeted age ranges is necessary to build effective games.

(pp. 316–317)[21]

The physical interface is one of the key developmental considerations when designing simulation-based learning experiences. While this aspect may be device-specific, how children connect with simulation will be dependent on their dexterity. In addition to these physical considerations, there are also conceptual issues that are affected by a student's developmental level. How can the student handle abstractions? Can the child identify relationships between phenomena within the simulated experience? How do students use strategic processing in less organized learning environments often found within simulations?

The next sections of this chapter will address the issues related to the physical, motor, social, cognitive, and emotional domains when using simulations, beginning with the physical and motor considerations.

PHYSICAL AND MOTOR DEVELOPMENTAL CONSIDERATIONS

The physical and motor interaction between children and the platforms and devices used to support simulations is important to consider, as motor skills tend to develop with age. The size of a device may make it prohibitive for students with smaller hands to hold. Younger students also tend to have a more difficult time manipulating devices, with challenges in accuracy, speed, and smoothness of movement with device inputs. Younger

Developmental Considerations of Simulations 73

children may also have a difficult time using simulations that require multiple physical actions. For example, when using augmented reality, they may be required to move in space while manipulating a hand-held device. A lack of these motor skills can affect success and engagement with the simulation, as students may find these challenges frustrating.

Miller and Kocurek found that there was little literature connecting the motor skills and visual acuity of young children and the usability of mobile devices; however, the ability to use a touchscreen seems to appear in 6-year-olds demonstrating increasing motor ability.[21] Being attentive to the challenges of tapping or dragging is important to note, and the simulation should be adjusted to student need. For example, 12-month-old children are rarely observed using swipe or drag movements; that skill moderately increases at 2 years.[44] At 12 months, actions with the full hand and multiple fingers are more prevalent; while at 2 years, taps and single-finger movements are observed more frequently.[21]

Simulation inputs are also important to consider when examining the appropriateness of particular simulations to be used with early adolescents (ages 5–10). As Radu, MacIntyre, and Lourenco noted:

> Children's augmented reality usability issues are potentially explainable by psychology areas such as motor skills (bimanual coordination, hand-eye coordination, fine motor skills, gross motor skills, endurance), spatial cognition (spatial memory, spatial perception, spatial visualization), attention (selective attention, divided attention, executive control), logical thinking (abstract vs. concrete thinking)

and memory (capacity and operations). These developmental factors are all undergoing development in young children, thus have the potential to influence how children react to augmented reality applications.

(p. 289)[45]

They examined the use of augmented reality simulations using hand-held devices with early adolescents. In an augmented reality game, students pointed a smartphone at a table with a game board. The device then created an augmented reality where they needed to collect objects by adjusting the position of the smartphone and making a selection by either tapping the object directly with their finger or positioning cross-hairs and engaging a collection command using a side button.

They found that students were statistically significantly faster when directly tapping an object as it appeared on a screen versus moving the device and using buttons on the device to collect the object with the cross-hairs. They were able to recover from errors with a similar speed and accuracy using both types of approaches. The speed that it took to accomplish the tasks and recover from errors decreased with age. Even though it took longer to accomplish the task with the younger students under both conditions, errors were not significantly different between the tasks or the age groups. However, students reported that using their finger to directly touch an on-screen object was easier to complete. Even though touching the screen was shown to be a quicker way to gather the objects, smaller students might find it difficult to hold the smartphone and tap the screen at the same time. Educators might make

COGNITIVE AND SOCIAL CONSIDERATIONS

Beyond being just a physical challenge, holding a device and simultaneously using its touchscreen might also be difficult for these children in a cognitive sense. Such important cognitive considerations might include: managing cognitive load, understanding task demand challenges within the simulation, coordinating multiple goals during activities, monitoring self-progress, and dealing with nontraditional cognitive strategies. To begin, cognitive load may be a challenge for some students, as the active nature of the outputs from simulations might inhibit learning. Overloading students with data, information, and images can challenge students' ability to glean what's important and what isn't. Augmented reality simulations require the student to integrate objects in the real world with those in virtual space. Being able to integrate the real and the virtual requires a level of cognitive sophistication that younger children may not yet have.

Students might also be challenged in understanding task demands within the simulation. Creating a well-organized experience may be better suited to help a student attempt to figure out what needs to be accomplished to be able to work strategically. For example, students may need to work to manage and coordinate multiple goals during activities. In a complex simulation like *SIMPOLICON*, students need to balance the goals of economic development, international relations, and environmental sustainability while serving as simulated leaders of a country. Meeting these goals may relate to one another, but they may also conflict, making it a challenge to find a good balance. A supportive instructional approach would be to encourage students to work through steps of exploration to help them understand the nature of the task to learn key concepts. These processes may require scaffolding that includes monitoring progress and providing informal and formal feedback from the teachers and peers.

Helping students monitor their self-progress is also an important consideration. The simulation may be very engaging but provide little opportunity for students to reflect upon their work. As mentioned in other sections, this aspect of the learning process requires the instructor to provide reflective structures (e.g., post-simulation questions, writing prompts) to provide time for students to think about their progress. A balance of teacher-led instruction and simulated experiences can help students assess their own learning.

Simulations often require nontraditional cognitive strategies. For example, traditional curriculum may not emphasize inquiry-based instruction. Providing younger students support during open-inquiry or open-discovery, where the student is free to explore the simulation with little guidance, is important in facilitating learning. In their review of digital applications used with preschool students, Ni and Yu found:

> [T]here are shortcomings with the [mobile games], which are: (1) As a special group, preschool children's cognitive thinking is still in its initial stages and the existing interaction interface is not in line with the cognitive characteristics

Developmental Considerations of Simulations

and cognitive habits of children, (2) The interfaces of education applications have too many layers and are too complex, which lack visual centers making them difficult for children to use, (3) The direct transfer of the traditional early education mode to the digital platform does not take full advantage of the platform's features and benefits.

(p. 166)[46]

This observation highlights the importance of understanding pre-school students' cognitive needs and the necessity for designing simulations with an attention to those needs. Using prompts to draw students' attention to pertinent simulated phenomena or making clearer where students were in an inquiry process may help support students. The role of curriculum developer and teacher are critical in finding the match between developmental level and digital application.

Using Piaget as a learning framework, Ni and Yu outlined the key developmental stages and how they relate to digital games for children ages 0–7:

> (1) Perceived action stage—games for practicing: In this type of game there is always a new function that needs to be mastered. (2) Pre-operation stage—symbolic games: It is the typical form of children's games, and is also the characteristic of self-centered games during the characterization activity period, which is that assimilation surpasses adaption and begins to dominate. Children establish contacts subjectively between signals and objects being signalized and organize activities without considering about specific things and the real environment.
>
> (p. 167)[46]

78 Developmental Considerations of Simulations

Based on these constructs, they recommended the following for children ages 3–7:

- Click, drag and drop is the most popular mode of operation at mobile devices. For preschool children, the multi-touch interactive mode of mobile devices should be designed more closely to daily life, such as click or drag with different visual and sound effects.
- Because [a child's] nervous system is not fully mature, they cannot focus for as long as adults. So when they have to stick to a job, feedback and reward should be given often and in a timely manner.
- Imitation is the main way for preschool children to learn. They imitate the behavior of others to grasp and study the experience of others.
- Prosocial behavior level grows with age. The study found that level of preschool children's prosocial behavior showed a trend of rising and enhanced performance for a sense of cooperation. (p. 168)[46]

And building upon Norman's (2005) work of design that includes the sensory, behavioral, and reflective components of children's interactions with games, Ni and Yu describe some key features to consider when creating games for younger children:

- In terms of sensual and intuitive experience: The hierarchy dictates that simple, intuitive and concrete images are often used; colors are usually those that can be commonly seen in daily life, such as warm colors and timely audio feedback to attract people's attention.

- In terms of specific functions: Learning step-by-step from simple functions to difficult ones so as to make progress; there are personification interactions throughout the game, and reminders are offered timely, creating an open-ended experience through free choices.
- In terms of final emotional goal: It is worth showing off to turn traditional receptive knowledge into expressive knowledge. (p. 168)[46]

Radu et al. also noted some critical software factors to consider when using simulations with small children.[45] During the object-gathering task, if the object was not in direct line of sight (hidden in virtual tunnels), students had a greater chance of losing track of the game board, requiring the student to reset the game. This situation also increased the number of errors accumulated when attempting to capture the objects; these errors accrued as a result of students' needi to move the device in a greater number of angles and positions around the game board. They would either move the device around the board or bend themselves while holding the device stationary, and both actions increased the chance that they might mis-aim the device. This situation might present a management challenge if the game resets, distracts, or frustrates students. Providing scaffolds like on-screen arrows to help direct students or warnings that the device is losing its tracking could be effective in preventing these conundrums. These features may be important factors for educators to keep in mind when deciding which simulation application is most appropriate for their students.

80 Developmental Considerations of Simulations

Literacy considerations are also important when using simulations with small children. Depending on the students' numeracy skills, simulations may need to be strictly qualitative; those using numbers, graphs, and numerical charts may be beyond the developmental skills of these small children. In their study using interview and observation data with parents and children, Chaudron et al. found that children's use of technology was mediated by their cognitive development, especially with respect to reading and writing skills. They asserted that children's technological skills were directly linked to development of their ability to read and write.[41] This means teachers must understand that their students' skills and challenges with simulation use are connected their skills and challenges with the more traditional academic subjects of math, reading, and writing.

Starting with pre-readers, it is important that simulations tap into children's experiences to find language that is in their productive vocabulary. As their language skills develop, consider using simulations with language that may be more familiar to them. This language may include home experiences (rooms in a house, objects around them) and actions (eating, sleeping). Incorporating familiar scenes and experiences may lower language barriers for younger children. Additionally, phrases and commands should be simplified, as Miller and Kocurek noted when discussing educational game design:

> In addition to the specific words that children are learning, the language [or text] used in the game should also be carefully constructed. For example, connecting words

Developmental Considerations of Simulations 81

> such as but, then, because, it, and so are typically in the repertoire after 30 months. For a younger child (i.e., 2-year-old), it might be challenging to understand the connecting words and string together the statements, ideas, and/or concepts. Thus, the mean length utterance should be limited to ensure easier connections by children.
>
> (p. 318)[21]

Keeping instructions and feedback in short phrases may be more developmentally appropriate for younger children. Additionally, pre-readers will need more instructions either offered in pictures or heavily mediated by the instructor through verbal prompts.

In working through learning and creating cognitive connections, Miller and Kocurek provided guidelines to help students:

> The child may need to figure out the correspondence between word (e.g., spoon) to the correct object (e.g., utensil). One strategy is to assess other cues in the environment; perhaps the word is accompanied with a gesture that indicates the location of the referent or perhaps the attentional focus of the individual indicates the direction of the referent.
>
> (p. 319)[21]

These cues may come from the game itself or through teacher mediation. When learning new language, there should be multiple familiar scenarios and tasks to help the student put the new terms in frameworks that already exist for the child.[28] In an example where an educational game is teaching the child about pears,

82 Developmental Considerations of Simulations

Miller and Kocurek discuss supporting this learning through the design of the game:

> [The new term] has been embedded in the environment and with enough exposure, the child will not only learn about pears but also the function and appropriate social skills regarding sharing. This example is in stark contrast to the flashcard method that plagues many of the educational systems.
>
> (p. 319)[21]

They highlighted the importance of students working with each other and the teacher to construct, ultimately, their own meaning using their own existing beliefs and understandings that are useful to help students develop understanding of concepts.

When working with older students, simulations provide both advantages and challenges to address. Simulations offer features to support adolescent learning similar to those specific to other age groups. Whether it is scaffolding content or supporting cognitive and metacognitive processing, simulation tasks can be structured to meet the developmental needs of adolescents.

Working with tenth-graders, Wang et al. looked at students learning kinematics using a combination of classroom instruction and simulations, hypothesizing that adding a dynamic component to physics instruction helps students better visualize and examine phenomena to develop a deeper conceptual understanding.[8] They found that students showed higher learning gains related to basic projectile motion using a desktop or touchscreen simulation versus using a touchscreen with

Developmental Considerations of Simulations 83

an ability to sense tilting. From these results, the authors hypothesized further that the more simplified inputs (touchscreen and mouse) helped students develop a deeper conceptual understanding because the tilting of the screen added additional physical and cognitive challenges. However, in looking at learning more advanced projectile concepts—applying the basic concepts to new situations—students working with the touchscreens and touchscreen with tilt sensors showed a higher level of understanding than those who worked strictly with the desktop simulation. The added ability to physically manipulate virtual objects through the motions of tilting the screen and touching the screen perhaps allowed students a more concrete connection to abstract phenomena. Interestingly, students with lower spatial ability did equally well with science concepts using the touchscreen and the touchscreen with the tilt sensor as their higher ability counterparts. However, there was a gap between ability levels when they used the desktop version of the simulation. For teachers working with adolescents, it is important to consider the physical and developmental needs, such as abilities to hold and manipulate devices, of students and make intentional choices in using hardware to support simulation experiences.

The social nature of interactions around simulations becomes important to help students develop the interpersonal and emotional skills necessary for learning outcomes. Miller and Kocurek described two broad types of social interaction to support this learning:

> During the sensitive response, the child plays a guiding role in leading the learning experience in the environment

while the social partner plays a more supportive role. On the other hand, during the redirective response, the child plays a more passive role while the social partner dictates the attentional focus.

(p. 320)[21]

In their support for student learning, the role for teachers and caregivers is to provide encouragement, as opposed to sharp correction, when working through difficult material. In a guiding role, the child is more active in their learning, while the teacher or caregiver provides feedback and guidance as needed. Scaffolding can include the teacher or caregiver asking questions about activities, drawing attention to particular aspects of the simulation, and offering gentle feedback if actions are off track.

For very young children, this social mediation is more effective with a person and live action, rather than feedback from a digital device or application. Children are more able to perform an action if they are able to see it live and then have a chance to repeat it. Incorporating live action into simulation participation may be a critical task to maximize learning with young children

While caregivers are increasingly concerned about screen time, the more important consideration is knowing what they are doing with the applications and how much the time is mediated by an adult to foster learning. For example, a tablet that is functioning as a *de facto* television to show entertainment is a different scenario than a child using the tablet to explore topics of history. Viewing applications together can be a method

Developmental Considerations of Simulations 85

to support this learning and foster caregiver-and-child social interaction. However, merely watching the material together does not maximize the learning potential; there should be an interaction component occurring along with the viewing. Miller and Kocurek described some of these supports, including from within the educational games—advice quite applicable to simulations as well. Those supports should be designed to the following: 1) encourage using dialogue and questioning at certain points in the game, 2) provide feedback to help the caregiver gauge the child's engagement, 3) provide ideas to help caregivers make connections between the game and the child's interests and needs, and 4) allow the caregiver to structure the game to tailor it to the child.[21]

Play can be an important component of educational games and simulations. Miller and Kocurek described how to balance educational aims while incorporating play:

> One way to achieve this is by creating an environment with guided exploration. Including fun and engaging activities in an open environment allows the child an opportunity and potential for creativity and imaginative play. The balance of semi-structured environments takes advantage of the demonstrated developmental processes that contribute to positive learning and developmental outcomes.
>
> (p. 325)[21]

In addition to these more individualized concerns about the social nature of learning, it is also important to note equity in the depiction of characters within games.

These avatars often serve as important role models for children and can run the risk of reinforcing stereotypes.

KEY TAKEAWAYS FROM THIS CHAPTER

Above all, take care to match the skills and understandings of students to the interface and outputs of the simulations. Research suggests that using multiple representations of phenomena helps in student learning, but it is important to manage students' cognitive loads.[18] Being attentive to how students are examining simulated representations of phenomena to make certain students are able to observe key aspects of that phenomena. As an example, if the most relevant task in a simulation activity is to identify a pattern in data, taking data "snapshots"—that is, taking away some of the "live" nature of the simulation by pausing it to prevent the creation of new data—may help illustrate a particular concept. In this case, if the simulation is too dynamic, students may be unsure on which details they should focus.

An important strength of some simulations is their ability to control the depth of the content and the order in which the topics are covered. The teacher can be intentional in how material is broken down into sub-components that might be easier for students to process. For example, an activity may require students to complete a task—say, measuring an object—before proceeding to the next part of the simulation, thereby inserting a kind of pause in which students can spend more time with part of the topic before moving on.[10]

Simulations may also allow teachers to differentiate instruction by using applications that use multiple levels

Developmental Considerations of Simulations

of interaction based upon a student's needs and interests. Educational games, like simulations, can be quite adaptable to students, as Gee noted:

> Good games confront players in the initial game levels with problems that are specifically designed to allow players to form good generalizations about what will work well later when they face more complex problems. Often, in fact, the initial levels of a game are in actuality hidden tutorials. Work in cognitive science has shown that people need to be presented with problems in a fruitful order, getting initial problems that set up good generalizations for later problems. If they are confronted too early with problems that are too complex, they often come up with creative solutions, but ones that turn out, in the end, not to be very helpful for working on other problems later on (Elman 1993). Good games don't do this, but order problems in helpful ways.
>
> (pp. 2–3)[31]

A major strength of both games and simulations is their ability to tailor the simulated experiences to the developmental level of the student.

Four

Facilitating Cognitive and Metacognitive Processes during Simulations

> When examining microeconomic principles, Mr. Davis' students are examining an economic simulation used to model the automobile market. In this simulation, students are comparing consumer preferences for hybrid-, diesel-, or gasoline-powered vehicles. Mr. Davis has asked the students to first explore the simulation to learn some basics about each type of vehicle (e.g., purchase cost, operating cost). Later in class, students "run" simulations by changing market conditions (e.g., cost of diesel fuel, price of batteries) to determine why consumers may choose one type of vehicle over another. Throughout the lesson, students are asked about their ideas and use evidence from the simulation to support these ideas. After the simulated experiences, Mr. Davis asks questions that determine whether students' explanations are useful in predicting the market share for each type of vehicle.

In the example above, Mr. Davis designed a simulation experience that is attentive to student cognition and metacognition. Students were asked to share ideas and use the simulation to explore and test these ideas. Within the lesson he was attentive to differing levels of cognitive and metacognitive processes to help students develop more sophisticated explanations (e.g., those that could predict).

The purpose of this chapter is to discuss the cognitive and metacognitive processes and strategies that may be facilitated through the use of simulations and how these processes may lead to more desirable learning outcomes. Both cognition and metacognition treat the student as active in their learning process. When talking about **cognition**, we are considering students' understanding of the subject matter itself. Strategies associated with cognition address how students learn about a concept or procedure. Cognition can be divided roughly into two categories: lower- and higher-order thinking. **Lower-order thinking** involves one step or action and can include activities like observing, noting, categorizing, or recording. **Higher-order thinking** requires the learner to do something with the information beyond that first step; these actions might include hypothesizing, predicting, generalizing, analyzing, or interpreting. Bloom's and Webb's taxonomies are useful when categorizing the types of cognitive activities that students are asked to do during classroom activities.

Metacognition refers to students' consciousness of their own thinking and how they go about that thinking. This kind of thinking incorporates specific strategies like considering previous approaches to a problem or asking for help. Metacognition also includes students' beliefs about their own learning. A student's metacognitive beliefs may include ruminations about how they learn best, what they feel they understand well, and what they have to work on.

These cognitive and metacognitive outcomes support the development of deeper understanding of content, and simulations aid in this process; as Smetana and Bell noted, "Computer technology allows for reflection and revision by presenting the opportunity to test, reflect on, and revise multiple hypotheses" (p. 1359).[20] When examining how cognition and metacognition relate to simulations, it is useful to consider some of the related outcomes or behaviors that can be observed when using these applications. This chapter will be organized into sections that address cognitive and metacognitive goals and processes and how they can be effectively supported using simulations. We will begin with cognition.

COGNITION

When thinking about cognition, we must consider how students acquire knowledge through their experiences. Cognitive goals may include deep understanding of subject areas, and this understanding will come from two avenues: formal and informal experiences. The informal experiences could include observations of the world at home, discussions about the world with family members, or impressions of the world gleaned from the media. More formal experiences are those that occur in formal settings, like school. These experiences might take the form of empirical investigations, activities with fellow students, or teacher-directed independent assignments. Simulations provide a unique experience when compared to other approaches. Since they can allow students the opportunity to explore spaces, data, human interactions, and phenomena in ways that the real-world cannot provide, thinking about how students attain new knowledge in these environments is critical. These experiences may be informal when the student explores on their own or more formal with teacher-directed simulation activities for the student to complete.

Cognitive and Metacognitive Processes 91

Strategies associated with cognition address how students learn about a concept or procedure. In Dinsmore and Zoellner's examination of cognitive strategies when working with an online climate change simulator called *C-LEARNS*, they categorized shallower strategies as the following: 1) controlling variables, 2) re-running/repeating a trial, 3) using a help feature, and 4) making a local restatement.[47] When students control variables in a simulation, they adjust one condition while keeping all other conditions the same. In a population simulation, this strategy means that students might keep immigration, birth and mortality rates constant, while allowing the emigration rate to increase, to see what effect the change might have on overall population size. When re-running or repeating a trial, students would run a simulated trial again, with the conditions the same, to see if the results repeat. Using a help feature within a simulation allows the student to seek a better understanding of the simulation, attempting to find out how the simulation functions or the definition of unfamiliar terminology. Finally, in a local restatement, the student describes the conditions or results from a trial. Using the population simulation example, a student might state that the population in a given country decreased after running a trial.

Students using deeper cognitive strategies with simulations can include the following: 1) cued history, 2) prediction, 3) question, 4) argument, 5) global restatement, and 6) interpretation or elaboration.[46] When using cued history strategies, students may change a variable to better understand a simulated outcome. An example might include increasing the immigration rate to understand the effect it has on overall population through time. Using this example, students may also incorporate a prediction strategy. They may guess that increasing immigration will increase overall country population in a given year. Students may question procedures, observations, or conclusions they have made. In this case, they might question whether immigration is the only factor at play when looking at population level. When using an arguing strategy, the student makes an argument about a particular simulated parameter. For example, they might argue that a population could be kept stable if you cut off all immigration, but they might consider this unrealistic, as most countries need some levels of immigration to serve workforce needs. In the global restatement strategy, students are able to summarize the findings from multiple trials to identify trends or comparisons between initial conditions and results. Finally, in the interpreting or elaborating cognitive strategy, a student interprets these trends or comparisons. In the population simulation example, students might observe that there is a balance point between immigration and mortality rates and interpret that phenomenon as what may keep a country's population stable.

Simulations help to foster these cognitive strategies, as noted by Squire et al. in their work with an electrostatics simulator:

> students in the experimental group were recalling experiences and challenges that were a part of the design of *Supercharged*, whereas, students in the control group were relying more on their ability to memorize information. Playing *Supercharged* enabled some students to

Cognitive and Metacognitive Processes

confront their conceptions of electrostatics, as they played through levels that contradicted their understandings. Students used *representations* of electric fields depicted in the game as *tools for action*. These initial findings suggest that the primary affordances of games as instructional tools may be their power for eliciting students' alternative misconceptions and then providing a context for thinking through problems. Adept game players appropriate game representations as tools for thinking, which, for some students . . . were later taken up in solving other physics problems."

(p. 518)[9]

As noted in the above example, students engage in multiple cognitive strategies while working through their confrontation with prior knowledge; those situations are what simulations can handily provide.

Simulations bring several cognitive challenges to which the teacher must be attentive. These challenges include students' ability to process the simulated phenomena within the simulation in order to make connections to other phenomena they encounter. Trouble performing these actions may be rooted in a difficulty taking multiple forms of information and pulling them together to create a coherent whole. For example, a simulation may present data describing climate that changes through time. Students might have a difficult time synthesizing different aspects of the phenomena, including tree planting, tree loss, temperature change, and atmospheric carbon dioxide levels, to create a coherent mental model that represents the actual phenomena. Students might make connections between tree planting and carbon dioxide levels, but they may not understand how those resulting connections relate to temperature changes.

Additionally, they may struggle with knowing what details to pay attention to within the simulation. There may be "flashy" components that draw the student's attention, but they don't help to develop conceptual understanding:

> learners frequently limit their attention to the most perceptually salient but not necessarily the most thematically relevant features of the visualisations, do not interact with them in a structured and goal-oriented way, and do not systematically relate the different sources of information to each other in order to construct a coherent mental representation.
>
> (p. 338)[18]

As students struggle to be systematic when working with simulations to solve a problem or develop a mental representation of the concept under investigation, the teacher has an important role in structuring tasks, connecting information, and overall helping students to focus on important features within the simulation.

To support learners when working with simulations, cues can help focus students' attention. If a goal for learning is to develop a conceptual model, helping students build that model in a step-by-step manner can provide a clear path to achieving that goal. In some cases, simulations provide complex and dynamic visualizations of phenomena. Allowing students to have the opportunity to view this phenomenon in a more static manner can help them develop a better understanding of the subject. Bodemer et al. argued that

> [t]hese support measures typically guide learners to (1) focus on specific variables of the underlying model, (2) generate hypotheses about relationships between these variables, (3) conduct simulated experiments in order to test the hypotheses, and (4) evaluate the hypotheses in light of the observed results. It has been demonstrated, however, that successful learning with interactive simulations requires further support. In particular, generating and testing hypotheses seem to be very demanding tasks.
> (p. 327)[18]

Bodemer et al. noted that working outside the simulated environment (e.g., using paper, participating in group discussions) can support pulling together different bits of information.[18] This work can include creating graphic organizers, argument charts, and concept maps to help students develop their integrated conceptual models.

METACOGNITION

Metacognition is concerned with the processes in which students consciously consider their own thinking and how they best learn.[48] In a broad sense of goals for these processes, we want students to be able to understand their own learning. Throughout schooling, teachers provide various levels of scaffolding to help students in this regard. Instructors might give prompts to encourage students to think about prior learning, teach strategies like note-taking to help students monitor how well they are processing information, or provide time and structures for students to reflect upon what they have learned.

Metacognitive goals include students being able to reflect upon and understand their learning for themselves. Scheoenfeld categorized these strategies as planning, checking, monitoring, selecting, revising, and evaluating.[49] When planning, students might outline the steps they will take when starting a task. An example would be a student planning to do background research on key events of the civil rights movement before deciding on a research topic related to the *Brown versus the Board of Education* Supreme Court decision. In checking and monitoring knowledge, students may consider where their ideas originate, whether they come from more formal academic activities or personal experiences. They may establish a sense of how much they think they know about a given topic. In the above example of the *Brown* decision, after reading about some key events from the civil rights movement, a student might determine that they need to learn about the legal justification of Jim Crow laws to develop an understanding of the laws behind having separate schools for African-American students and white students.

Additional metacognitive strategies might include creating a sketch or diagram to summarize their thinking about a concept, taking notes during a lecture, or developing a physical model to represent an idea. For the *Brown* decision activity, students might create a timeline of critical events to put key concepts relating to the decision in a temporal context. Monitoring strategies might include asking questions, noting when they seem to understand an idea, and having a sense of their progress in the course of completing a learning task. As an example, students might note that they understand some of the key terms of an *amicus* brief and how it relates to the *Brown* case. When evaluating learning, students might share the reasoning behind their ideas.

These processes related to metacognition can be supported through both simulations and active teacher involvement. Prompts can be used at various points of a simulated experience to ask students to reflect upon their experiences. The teacher can also help students by teaching reflective strategies as they work through the simulation.

Using Dinsmore and Zoellner's typology of metacognitive strategies, observable metacognitive outcomes include students 1) sharing their metacognitive knowledge, 2) reporting their metacognitive experiences, and 3) setting goals. Using their metacognitive knowledge, a student might state their extant knowledge and beliefs and how they might affect their decision-making within a task. For example, when working with a flight simulator, a student would state that they have seen movies that state that it is important to keep the plane's nose up when landing and that they will try to do that when they work with the simulator. When reporting their metacognitive experiences, students share what they are experiencing in the simulator and how this might affect a decision. In the flight simulator example, a student might notice that even though they are increasing airspeed, they are losing altitude. They would take a few moments to look at other gauges to decide what to do next. Finally, students can set goals

Cognitive and Metacognitive Processes

as a metacognitive strategy. In the flight simulator, they state they are going to take the plane to the highest altitude possible to see what effects it might have on the dynamics of the plane.

Again, the key metacognitive strategies, as delineated by Scheoenfeld, include planning, checking, monitoring, selecting, revising, and evaluating. Simulations may facilitate these kinds of strategies as can be seen in the following examples. Returning to our example of *Supercharged*, students have opportunities to use these metacognitive strategies. The goal for the students is to place electrostatic charges in a maze that will either help or impede the progress of a simulated spaceship. Prior to each level, students are given time to plan and place the charges where they think will allow the ship to make it through the maze. During the simulation, students can check and monitor progress through the maze, make adjustments to the charges of the particles, and monitor fuel levels in the ship. Based on whether they met the goal, students can revise their plan to re-run their trial.[9]

Educators need to be attentive to the several metacognitive challenges that students using simulations can face. These include

> in simulation environments for discovery learning, learners attempt to infer the structure of an underlying conceptual model by changing the values of input variables in a static or dynamic way and by observing the consequences of these changes in the presented symbolic and pictorial representations. However, many learners do not interact with the presented external representations in a

structured and goal-oriented way and fail to formulate, test, and evaluate hypotheses systematically.

(p. 326)[18]

KEY TAKEAWAYS FROM THIS CHAPTER

Simulations have been touted to support model-based instruction advocated by the NRC and *Next Generation Science Standards*.[50] Teachers can design simulated experiences that foster cognitive strategies by asking students to discuss their prior knowledge, make predictions, and discuss their findings. While a strength of simulations might be in providing experiences that are more accessible to students, they may need assistance in how best to process and reflect upon the information they are taking in. One critical component of supporting metacognitive thinking requires intervention on the teacher's part. As students work with the simulations, they need space and assistance to find ways to process the information they interact with and reflect upon their experiences. As noted in the previous section, supports that are reflective of a student's cognitive developmental level must be in place for metacognitive processing to occur.

Simulations can provide support for both cognitive and metacognitive goals; however, the instructor still has an important role. First, in the process of selecting the appropriate simulation, the instructor should select a simulation that contains supports or space for prompts that incorporate metacognitive strategies, prompts that allow students to assess their current understanding. Even with these prompts, the teacher may need to teach processing skills such as how to plan when working within the simulations. Absent these supports, the teacher may need to provide them instead with supplementary materials or instruction.

In their work with a climate change simulation, Dinsmore and Zoellner noted two implications for science teachers that can be applied to other domains:

> First, science teachers should ensure that their students are exposed to a wide variety of strategies. Simply teaching the history-cued strategy does not appear to result in students building complex conceptions of science topics, such as global warming. In other words, teachers should be attuned to the patterns of strategy use, rather than just the frequency or types of strategies utilized. One way to help students better understand their own patterns of strategy use is through supporting students to continually monitor their progress and employ strategies that are appropriate for their level of understanding, which should result in a better understanding of complex, scientific phenomena.
>
> Second, teachers should be attuned to the other factors that predict optimal patterns of strategy use. In this case, topic interest was particularly salient in this regard as it appears to be key for students' metacognitive and cognitive development. This may be particularly important as topic interest was highly related to all three forms of strategies (i.e., surface, deep, and metacognitive), and use of all three strategies was important for the higher performers.
>
> (p. 113)[47]

Five

Simulations in the Domains

> The explosion of digital technology has created a revolution similar to the "hands-on" movement of the 1960s. The flexibility, speed, and storage capacity of contemporary desktop computers is causing science educators to redefine the meaning of hands-on experience and rethink the traditional process of teaching. The challenge facing both science educators and science teacher educators is to evaluate relevant applications for information technologies in the science curriculum. At the same time, instruction utilizing information technologies must reflect what is known about the effectiveness of student-centered teaching and learning.
>
> (p. 39)[51]

Writing back in 2000, Flick and Bell recognized the burgeoning use of digital technology to transform science education. Notions of what it meant to be "hands-on" evolved from using laboratory equipment toward thinking about how students engaged in scientific processes to learn science. "Cookbook" lab activities were to be replaced with learning opportunities that allowed students to be engaged in data collection and theoretical model building. While digital simulations may take students out of the physical laboratory environment, they still provide an opportunity for students to engage in scientific processes and develop their own deeper understanding of science concepts. However, as noted earlier, the pedagogical, developmental, and cognitive and metacognitive considerations of these simulated experiences can be as important as the sophistication of the simulation technology.

Each domain has applications of simulations for the classroom; as one might expect, though, they tend to be best served with different types of simulations, although there may be overlap of functionality and purpose of the simulation exercise. The nature of the objectives and goals for each domain will dictate which kind of simulation is most appropriate. Some emphasize virtual or human interaction, some simulate complex systems that can be modified or manipulated to examine outcomes based on these changes, and some offer simplified models that represent a real-world phenomenon. And, of course, the social fields are interested in data just as the sciences are concerned about human interactions.

Complex human interaction, such as motivation in markets or tensions caused by social systems, may be understood though effective use of simulations. Examples of these simulations include *Virtual City Planning*, *Crystal Island*, and *SIMPOLICON*. What makes these applications unique is their ability to quickly connect students in an internal scenario and to push them to reflect upon their experiences. The concepts are made more real for the students through various simulated activities.

Complex systems across the domains—ecosystems or financial systems, perhaps—may be made more understandable through simulations. Students can attempt to modify starting conditions or change variables as the system operates to see the effects of these modifications.

Finally, representations of complex phenomena across the domains may be made more accessible to students through simulations using different structures and processes. For example, there may be more of a focus on interactional data among human actors in the social studies. In mathematics, the simulation might be more about providing a visualization of an algorithm. In science, the focus might be on data analysis and investigation design. The structure of the domain and associated objectives dictate what the most appropriate simulation might be.

Each discipline has content and process goals that make up domain content knowledge, and both the content and process goals are meant to work together to support learning. For example, students may learn about literature by using the practices of literary critiques. Simulations can allow students the opportunity to engage in domain practices (critiques) while working with authentic information (historical texts). Using curriculum documents like the National Council for Teachers of Mathematics Standards, the *Common Core*, the *Next Generation Science Standards*, and the National Social Studies Standards provide both the content and process goals for each domain.

The chapter will be organized by the core domains found within typical K-12 curricula. For purposes here, the focus will be on language arts, mathematics, science, and social studies. The main reason for this focus is that these domains contain topics covered in most schools and are addressed in most states' assessments.

While this primary focus creates a crude determination of which domains to address, it accounts for most of the courses that students will encounter. To ameliorate this shortcoming, a section will be devoted to simulations that may address domains outside these core subjects. Each domain section will be examined with pedagogical, developmental, and cognitive and metacognitive considerations, as examined in the previous chapters. The curriculum constructs described in national documents will provide the lens when examining simulations used for these domains.

SIMULATIONS ACROSS THE DOMAINS

When examining simulations and their relationships with subject matter domains, it is important to define some of the terms under consideration. One of the primary areas of focus in this examination is how simulations support **domain knowledge**, defined as the critical understandings and information that students must have to understand the subject.[48] In looking at domain knowledge, each subject area contains content and process goals.

Content goals address the core knowledge and frameworks that serve the discipline. For example, knowledge goals in the history curriculum might be an ability to name the relevant Supreme Court cases that address the First Amendment's establishment clause. Additionally, each discipline may have goals that address the primary frameworks used by disciplinary experts. Continuing to use the previous example, to show expertise in using primary historical frameworks, students may need to understand the relevant First Amendment cases in the framework of the principle of the separation of church and state and how the Supreme Court has applied this concept at various times in history. These goals are meant to equip students with the essential information and conceptual framings attributed to those who have expertise in the field.

Process goals focus on how knowledge and theories are generated within the domains. For example, in science students may engage in processes associated with scientific inquiry to help learn content. These processes can include posing research questions, generating and examining data, and, using logic and imagination, developing explanations to answer these research questions or explain the phenomenon under consideration. Students in a social studies class may use similar processes but examine information or data that is more relevant to the domain, such as primary source documents. Students in these courses might analyze the Federalist Papers to better understand the origins and intentions of the Bill of Rights or look at immigrants' letters back to their home countries to find first-person perspectives on the process of immigration through Ellis Island upon entering the United States. In these cases, students need to show expertise in the processes that scientists and historians use.

Both content and process goals are meant to work synergistically in most domains. Engaging these practices in the classroom is designed to provide students a sense of how practitioners—historians, mathematicians, linguists—work (process), while helping them learn domain knowledge (content). Digital applications then can be designed to support each of these categories of goals when students work within their simulated environments. Students can examine images of primary source documents for history, simulated data in math and science, and collected writing samples in English language arts. Instructors can support this work by giving students prompts for questions, noting key features of the information being analyzed, and aiding in drawing conclusions. This scaffolding can occur with varying degrees of detail to match the skill and developmental levels of students.

To help understand how simulations can support domain knowledge, examples will be used throughout the next sections. These examples will be organized by domain: language arts, mathematics, science, and social studies. In each of these sections, we will discuss the domain knowledge goals drawn from the key national documents guiding curricula at the national level. These documents were developed by representative committees consisting of members from educational, political, corporate, and domain-specific fields (e.g., historians, mathematicians, writers, scientists) in order to build a consensus around learning goals. In a broad sense, all of these documents support outcomes that focus on both an understanding of processes and content that exists within the frameworks of the domains (e.g., history, literary analysis, economics, biology, statistics). They advocate for reform of education that moves beyond strictly fact-based, declarative knowledge to a mix of process-and content-oriented goals. Then examples of simulations will be analyzed based on how they support these goals. Each domain group will also be examined with pedagogical, developmental, and cognitive and metacognitive considerations.

While these sections are organized into domains, many of the simulations examined involve concepts that might be applied to more than one single subject matter topic. For example, *Virtual City Planner*, included in the social studies domain section, could be used to reinforce environmental science concepts. In many cases, the richness of the simulation allows the educator much latitude to apply the experience to multiple domains.

LANGUAGE ARTS LEARNING GOALS

The *Common Core State Standards* for language arts is organized with multiple "anchor" strands to incorporate college and career texts with an eye toward proficiency in reading, writing, speaking and listening, and language.[52] To be proficient in reading, students need to be able to understand what is written, pull meaning from the text, understand the text's structure and perspective, and integrate knowledge and ideas found within the text. Working within varying contexts and constraints, students should be able to write for different purposes, understand and engage in an effective writing process, and use a research process to build and present knowledge. To show proficiency in speaking and listening, students should be able to comprehend and collaborate within conversations with differing groups and present ideas using varying media in a way that others can understand. Finally, within the anchor standards for language, students should be able to follow the conventions of language (e.g., grammar, structure), the contextual meaning of language, and the correct use of vocabulary. By design, these standards

HOW SIMULATIONS SUPPORT DOMAIN LEARNING GOALS IN THE LANGUAGE ARTS

As Halverson and Steinkuehler noted, the game-based simulations that are most effective depend on the aspect of literacy on which the teacher is focusing.[15] Educational games can provide students with an opportunity to effectively learn decoding and grammar skills; however, many of these games, specifically those consisting of puzzles and matching challenges, may not be considered simulations, as they are more drill-and-practice games. If they center on these skills only, they are not effective in addressing literacy issues that are related to context and social discourse.

To support the social nature involved in learning literacy skills, forums can provide space for students to engage with others and practice a social discourse. Rubio-Tamayo et al. noted the potential for virtual reality to serve as a support for student expression:

> Thus, [virtual reality] is a technology that in some way, simulates real world components, but it can also represent abstract or non-figurative ideas such as data or metaphors. Representation of ideas and concepts is another emerging line of research related to the application of virtual reality to some domains, considering that [virtual reality] has the potential to develop its own language and represent not only figurative components but also abstract ideas and metaphors.
>
> (p. 8)

They went on to say:

> Virtual reality and immersive environments imply a fictional narrative which can help us to represent otherwise our perception of the real world, in order to conceive and design new symbolic structures and cultural ensembles.
>
> (p. 9)[11]

As an example of an immersive simulation that could incorporate English domain skills, consider *Alien Contact!*, which was designed to address language arts, math, and scientific literacy skills for middle and high school students. Using GPS-enabled hand-held computers, students engaged in a narrative-driven, inquiry-based augmented reality simulation to connect students' real-world location with their virtual location in the simulation's digital environment. Students were given a scenario where aliens had landed on Earth and were preparing for an unknown action that could include peaceful contact, invasion, plundering, or returning to their home planet. In teams of four, students were tasked with exploring the augmented reality by interviewing virtual characters, collecting digital objects, and solving math, language arts, and scientific puzzles to determine why the aliens have landed. (p. 10)[10]

MATHEMATICS DOMAIN LEARNING GOALS

Domain learning goals for mathematics are defined by multiple documents at the national level, including *Principles and Standards for School Mathematics* and the *Common Core State Standards*.[52] Congruent with Alexander's theory of domain knowledge, key areas of focus include process (how knowledge is gained) and content (the knowledge in a particular subject) standard.[48] According to the *Principles and Standards for School Mathematics*, content areas include numbers and operations, algebra, geometry, measurement, and data analysis and probability. The processes related to the understanding of mathematical concepts include problem solving, reasoning and proof, communication, connections, and representations. These processes are similar to those advocated by the *Common Core State Standards* related to making sense of problem solving:

- Reason abstractly and quantitatively
- Construct viable arguments and critique the reasoning of others
- Model with mathematics
- Use appropriate tools strategically
- Attend to precision
- Look for and make use of structure
- Look for and express regularity in repeated reasoning[52]

HOW SIMULATIONS SUPPORT DOMAIN LEARNING GOALS IN MATHEMATICS

The *Rice Virtual Lab* in Statistics provides an online textbook, animated sample populations to generate data, case studies for examination, and demonstrations of key statistical concepts to promote learning in the subject. Students can manipulate conditions to generate data that they can then examine and visualize analyses of these data. In an approach called "query first," Lane and

Peres had college statistics students complete a pre-test to determine their ideas around a statistical concept.[36] Students then used a simulation to test those ideas and explore the accepted statistical concept. While the application provided support instruction, the students took the lead in exploring the simulation. The researchers found that this control helped keep students more focused and allowed them to challenge their existing conceptions. After the simulation work, students completed questions that the instructor provided to give their feedback.

Virtual reality may be useful in geometry as a way to examine spatial relationships[11]; furthermore, embodied cognition through gestures has had some positive application in mathematics.[53] Using gesture-based interfaces with simulations, students can work within a more abstract simulated experience while also engaging in concrete behaviors.

Authentic problems can be recreated and examined using simulations. Alibali and Nathan described their work with a simulation in which middle school mathematics students engaged in a remodeling project. Through this design work, the project incorporated student learning of geometry concepts.[54]

Steinkuehler & Duncan observed how forums could promote some of the domain's process goals found in the *Common Core State Standards*.[55] Students collaborated with each other to solve problems, use evidence to debate questions, and build mathematical models to make predictions about game-play. The social nature of these forums facilitated a social constructivist learning framework and helped students in the domain learning goal of understanding how mathematical peers work together to solve problems.

SCIENCE DOMAIN LEARNING GOALS

When examining the domain learning goals for science, *Science for All Americans*, the *National Science Education Standards*, the *Benchmarks for Science Literacy, Framework for K-12 Science Education*, and the *Next Generation Science Standards* provide a framework for delineating those goals.[56] [57] [58] [59] [60] The authors of these documents advocated for approaches that include teaching through inquiry, where students are active learners through posing questions, examining data and finding patterns therein, and creating explanations, or solutions, to various issues. They also include a call for teachers to use scientific processes such as helping their students develop models that explain scientific phenomena. An example of this approach is the *Modeling for Understanding in Science Education* Earth-Moon-Sun curriculum. Here students pose questions like: Why do we experience seasons? Using physical representations, students devise explanatory models to explain phenomena associated with the seasons.[61] Students share these models, and then revise them based on feedback from peers. This curriculum is designed to support process-oriented aspects of science while students learn declarative knowledge related to near-space astronomy.

Teaching in a manner promoted by these documents also pushes for students to investigate questions that are relevant to their community and bring their understanding to bear when devising solutions to these questions. One example could include striking a balance between the positive economic impact of expanding shipping in a city with the needs of a suitable habitat for wildlife within the local watershed.

HOW SIMULATIONS SUPPORT DOMAIN LEARNING GOALS IN THE SCIENCES

The directives above can create challenges for teachers, as it might be difficult to find the kinds of curriculum to support this instructional approach. Simulations provide a useful tool for teachers to enact the content and process goals described above. In the National Research Council report, *Committee on Science Learning: Computer Games, Simulations, and Education*, Honey and Hilton stated:

> Simulations and games have great potential to advance multiple science learning goals, including motivation to learn science, conceptual understanding, science process skills, understanding of the nature of science, scientific discourse and argumentation, and identification with science and science learning.
>
> (p. 25)

However, with this promise, they went on to say that there is little research to help educators understand the effects of simulations in science teaching:

> Most studies of simulations have focused on conceptual understanding, providing promising evidence that simulations can advance this science learning goal. There is moderate evidence that simulations motivate students' interest in science and science learning, and less evidence

about whether they support other science learning goals. Evidence for the effectiveness of games for supporting science learning is emerging but is currently inconclusive. To date, the research base is very limited.

(p. 2)[16]

While the research base is limited, a theme that should be clear from this book is that simulations cannot replace, or be a substitute for, well-designed and implemented instruction. This point is made clear by Dickes, Sengupta, Farris, Voss, and Basu in their work using simulations with elementary school students:

> [I]nquiry using simulations builds on, and/or complements inquiry activities that children conduct using other forms of modeling such as embodied modeling, as well as generating inscriptions (e.g., drawing and graphs). The path leading to agent-based models of emergent phenomena needs to be *designed*—it cannot simply be assumed that putting a child in front of the simulation may suffice to support her or his inquiry.
>
> (p. 771)[62]

To support the content domain goals in science, the *Virtual Cell Animation Collection* provides animations of cellular activities to facilitate the learning of the structure, function, development, and evolution of cells for college-level introductory biology courses.[63] The design of these presentations is to help students better visualize processes that are often presented statically and in two dimensions. This collection of animations can help instructors show the relationships between the various cellular structures during important processes (e.g., transcription and translation). While the simulated processes have been designed with enough detail for advanced biology college students, the instructor still has the power to highlight what is most relevant to the audience with whom they are working. The developers of this collection advocate scaffolding by the instructor.

The simulation's level of sophistication need not be a limit to the kinds of reactions and responses that can be garnered from using these platforms. While created in the mid-1990s and currently unavailable for current OS platforms, the *Genetics Construction Kit* provides a good example of how a simple simulation can lead to students' complex thinking about science. This software allowed students to "run" crosses of fruit flies.[64] Based on the offspring from these crosses, teams of students attempted to find patterns in the data to develop explanatory models to account for the offspring the crosses produced. These models needed to meet criteria that scientists often use to assess the qualities of their own models, including, among other things, explaining the data and having predictive power. As students work through different sets of genetic crosses, new patterns emerge that may be more complex—multiple alleles or codominance, perhaps—that require modifications and adaptations to their models. Throughout this process, students can present these models for their colleagues to examine and provide input that might require greater modification of their model to account for new data.[65] While the interface of this simulation would not be considered sophisticated by today's standards, the type of student inquiry it allowed proved to be quite complex and allowed students to engage in many key scientific processes, including data pattern recognition, explanatory model building, and scientific argumentation, while learning the genetics concepts of incomplete dominance and multiple alleles.

To foster an understanding of the social nature of science, online forums can provide spaces for students to engage in many of the scientific practices that fall in line with the process goals set forth by the National Research Council and the *Next Generation Science Standards*. As an example of how simulations can support some of the process domain goals in science, Adams found that college physics students were able to learn some of the norms of scientific practice through simulations.[19] Using *FoldIt*, game participants worked to predict how a protein's primary structure folded in three dimensions. Working with scientists, they were able to contribute to publications within *Nature* magazine, thus

> with each publication listing not only the scientists involved but the gamers as well, shifting the locus of scientific discovery from the expert in the lab to a network of professional-amateurs working in distributed fashion only through the context of a game, presenting an intriguing new model of not only civic participation in science.
>
> (p. 380)[15]

Moving beyond supporting science as citizens or laypeople, participants were able to take a step toward being contributors to the scientific enterprise through their work with game-based simulations.

SOCIAL STUDIES LEARNING GOALS

The National Council for the Social Studies defined the social studies domain learning goals through the publication *National Curriculum Standards for Social Studies*.[65] The council identified ten themes: 1) Culture, 2) Time, Continuity, and Change, 3) People, Places, and Environments, 4) Individual Development and Identity, 5) Individuals, Groups, and Institutions, 6) Power, Authority, and Governance, 7) Production, Distribution, and Consumption, 8) Science, Technology, and Society, 9) Global Connections, and 10) Civic Ideals and Practices.[66]

HOW SIMULATIONS SUPPORT DOMAIN LEARNING GOALS IN SOCIAL STUDIES

Simulations provide opportunities for social science educators to support both content and process domain learning goals. Much as they do in the other domains, they allow spaces where students can experience simulated phenomena to make social science concepts more real and/or authentic. While discussing physical simulations, many of the ideas noted below by Shellman and Turan, can apply to digital simulations:

> In short, [the simulation] facilitates the development of critical and analytical thinking and problem-solving skills. Our design also fosters understanding of negotiation processes and dynamics evident in international relations and various international organizations. Moreover, it facilitates understanding and analysis of countries' and organizations' societies, economies, and foreign policies. We elaborate on these points below and

> explain how our simulation aids in accomplishing the goals we set.
>
> (p. 21)[67]

Simulations—and here we refer to both physical and digital simulations—allow students the opportunity to examine aspects of the evolving nature of culture and political and economic power in ways that aren't easily accessible in a static textbook. With little risk associated in "messing up," since simulations can be designed to speed up processes, to be re-run, and to minimize social discomfort, students can work to create solutions for problems that are unfamiliar to them. Simulations can put students into situations that world leaders might face, which makes the debates, discussions, and solutions seem more real and substantive. As noted by Shellman and Turan above, simulations allow students to experience dynamics not available in case studies.

Simulations also allow students the chance to "try on" specific roles found in society. For example, in *Virtual City Planner*, they can make decisions about zoning to better understand how these actions affect neighborhoods and the environment. In *SIMPOLICON*, from the Akwaaba Foundation, students assume the various roles of world leaders to create policy that can affect the economic development, international relations, and environmental sustainability of the country of their choice.

Simulations also offer a tremendous opportunity to facilitate place-based learning pedagogies—students can connect social studies concepts to specific places and see how the sense of place can give them a specific perspective that historians employ in their practice. An example of this type of social studies application is *Jewish Time Jump: New York*, which is set in Washington Square Park and Greenwich Village in New York City.[68] This mobile simulation could be used with smartphones and tablets and allows users to visit several sites in Manhattan. The simulation was designed for fifth- through seventh-graders through an augmented reality experience to explore how under-represented populations contributed to history in the early 20th century. This application centered on the contributions of women of various ethnicities to the labor and suffrage movements, and the relationship of past events to current events, and can aid in the development of students more prepared to participate as citizens in a pluralistic society.[69] Students take on the role of reporters who travel through time to create a history of events around the Uprising of 20,000 labor strike, the Triangle Shirtwaist Factory fire, and the reforms that followed (organization of labor, voting rights for women). Students were able to witness events, interact with various historical figures, and examine primary source documents. After these experiences, students can then compare the events of the past to current labor struggles. This interaction with the past, simulated as it is, is designed to make the historical more personal, which could allow students to take a self-reflexive turn, highlighting how the current events can play a part in their consumer choices.[69] For example, there were complaints and suicides due to the working conditions within a factory of a manufacturer of many of the students' smartphones.[70] Additionally, in a much-debated program, the same company was given government incentives to move to Wisconsin.[71]

Dow Day provides another application, created for use in high school social studies classes, that incorporates a sense of place in the examination of past events.[72] It addressed the history around the university student protests, and the police reaction to these protests, during Dow Chemical recruitment efforts on the University of Wisconsin-Madison campus in the late 1960s. Students act as reporters to gather information while using GPS technology to connect with images and video clips of key moments of the protest. The simulation is designed to help students gather varying perspectives of an historical event.

OTHER AREAS OF SIMULATION FOCUS

While each domain can vary in approach and focus, some issues can be more integrative and connect multiple domains. For example, engineering problems tend to appear across such domains as math, science, and technology. The real-world focus of engineering challenges also can be more engaging to students, as opposed to simply reading about them in textbooks. For example, the Teachers Integrating Engineering into Science (TIES) program allows teachers to work with challenges involving a hot air balloon, a bumper car, and a bridge; the application is geared to work with middle school children to practice engineering processing while learning science content.[32] These concepts included a focus on structure and function, an iterative design process, cooperation within teams, and cooperative learning designs.

While simulations have advanced a great deal in the STEM areas, virtual reality has applications useful in creating art, likely making it useful in art instruction, as noted by Rubio-Tamayo et al.:

> [Virtual reality and immersive environments] are also conceived as technologies and media, and an emerging field for research in artistic creation and experimentation. They are not only an interactive and immersive canvas for representing ideas but also a dynamic tool for creation in a 3D space. The expressive and interactive power and multidimensional approach lead to innovation in creating and developing 3D environments.
>
> (p. 9)[11]

Specific art and media applications include *Tiltbrush*, *Infectious Ape*, and *Dear Angelica*.

TAKEAWAYS FROM THIS CHAPTER

Simulations hold much promise for integration in today's classroom. However, by the time this book is published, the specific technologies will be at least 1-year-old. There has to be a way to examine technology as it emerges that endures this ever-shifting landscape. Discussing science education, Flick and Bell noted some key guidelines to using technology in the classroom:

1. Technology should be introduced in the context of science content.
2. Technology should address worthwhile science with appropriate pedagogy.

3. Technology instruction in science should take advantage of the unique features of technology.
4. Technology should make scientific views more accessible.
5. Technology instruction should develop students' understanding of the relationship between technology and science. (p. 40)[51]

While their focus was on science education, these guidelines could be applied across domains, and be used for simulations specifically.

Teaching with simulations will require changes in the preparation of pre-service teachers and the professional development of in-service teachers. It might be tempting to provide experiences for both pre- and in-service teachers to work with the latest and greatest in simulation technology, and this idea is not an inherently bad one. These educators should be aware of the technology at least and have the opportunity to work with it in authentic classroom settings at best. But this action is not enough. As noted throughout this book, the teacher, as curriculum developer and implementer, is required to take an intentional, and often active, role in the instructional process. Depending on learning frameworks, pedagogical approaches, domain, topic, and developmental levels of students, the educator's role will need to be flexible and varied. Teacher preparation and professional development will be required to facilitate a deep understanding of these considerations and the role they play in the use of simulation.

Additionally, educators will need to be prepared to be well-informed consumers of simulation technology.

Just as there are many lesson plans of varying quality to be found on the web, so are there many simulation activities that are available and actively promoted. Some of the promotion is hype, with the technology failing to live up to the promises made by advertisements or salespeople. It is important for educators to be able to filter the noise to find those quality applications that will best serve their purposes. Even the best quality simulations must still be a good fit for the context of the school, the students, the teaching approach, and the accepted frameworks for understanding each domain. Preparation and professional development must help teachers understand how to sift through the hype and find the best technology for their classrooms.

FINAL REMARKS

In his examination of the post-Sputnik science education reform efforts, historian Rudolph noted the power that curriculum designers placed on film:

> By the 1950s, researchers in education and psychology saw film as a powerful means of addressing the shortage of qualified science teachers. Henry Chauncey, the president of Educational Testing Service and soon-to-be member of the PSSC Steering Committee, made the argument that the ideal solution to this problem "would be to have fewer teachers than at present and utilize them to better advantage than we now do." In the matter of imparting knowledge to students, Chauncey claimed that "instructional films can do as good a job in this respect—if not better—than the average classroom teacher." In this way, the very "best teachers in the country" could be produced at will, and the celluloid

> distributed wherever needed. . . . The primary pedagogical task, the conveyance of content, in this scheme would be "given over, in effect, to the experts who prepare the instructional films . . . and accessory materials."
>
> (p. 96)[73]

In this view, instructional films could be used as a means to address ineffective science instruction, supplanting the physical teacher with a bit of technology. With regard to simulations, though, this view, as noted by many studies, is not applicable. The role of the curriculum designer and teacher are critical when designing effective digital simulation experiences; the technology can no longer be a stand-in for the instructor.

If there is only one takeaway from this book, it is that simulation technology cannot replace good curriculum design and instruction. The nature of that instruction will need to change, but educators will continue to have an important role when working with simulations. The idea that students can be placed in front of a computer and deep learning will occur on its own, without designed curriculum and instruction, fails to fully leverage the potential of this technology.

Fads will always be part of the educational experience. With all new methods, approaches, policies, equipment, etc., nothing is more effective than solid educators developing strong relationships with their students and connecting the material to their needs and interests. Simulations allow a unique possibility for both teacher and student to take a novel perspective on learning.

As the technology around digital simulations and learning continues to emerge and evolve, it is important to reconsider the nature of educational research. New data-gathering techniques like eye- and motion-tracking technology provide a different kind of information to researchers. These techniques are made possible by simulations themselves—children interacting with a desktop computer naturally allows for the same computer to track eye movement. However, simulation technology also makes this type of data-gathering technology *necessary*—if movement is an important component of the simulation experience, the researcher will need to gather information about this movement.

The emerging technology requires a deep sense of how the children are learning and what supports are necessary to maximize this learning. More traditional approaches, augmented by the more innovative methods, will be important as the research agenda moves forward. Additionally, support, whether it is from teachers, from peers, or within the simulation, is seen as a critical factor in deepening student learning when using this technology. Continued research into the role of these supports will also need to continue to be part of the research agenda, but the field seems ripe for investigation.

Glossary

Augmented reality or mixed reality applications simulations that incorporate some real-world aspects (e.g., movement in physical space, a connection to a specific location, enhanced images), while providing various simulated aspects (e.g., illustrated characters or objects, information, modification of real-world images).

Authentic assessment a form of assessment meant to mirror real-world tasks, can support this view of student understanding.

Cognition students' understanding of the subject matter itself. Strategies associated with cognition address how students learn about a concept or procedure.

Content goals address the core knowledge and frameworks that serve a discipline (e.g., mathematics, science, English, social studies).

Designed experiences using simulations and educational games allows the learning experience to be treated less as a black box, bringing the learning process out in the open. Being attentive to both the design of inputs—the

Glossary 127

	simulation activities—and the outputs—how learning is assessed—is key to understand to understand how simulations can most effectively aid learning.
Digital games	applications that typically have rules and parameters, require the user to work toward achieving an outcome and provide status reports on progress toward this outcome.
Digital simulation	interactive software or web-based technology that provides students with experiences meant to mimic phenomena in the real world.
Domain knowledge	defined as the critical understandings and information that students must have to understand the subject
Embodiment	is the nature and amount of movement required by the participant to provide input to the simulation.
Gesture-controlled interfaces	some mobile hardware contains motion sensors that allow students the ability to provide input simply by moving the device. In this kind of hardware, input is given through student movement (e.g., hand, head, arms).
Higher-order thinking	requires the learner to do something with the information beyond that first step; these actions might include hypothesizing, predicting, generalizing, analyzing, or interpreting.
Input devices	allow the user to interact with the simulation in a tactile way; these devices can include a keyboard, mouse, and gesture-tracking devices.

Glossary

Interactivity — describes the nature of both the inputs given by students (e.g., mouse, gesture-tracking software) and the outputs from the devices in response to these inputs. Outputs can include sounds, visuals, and haptics (e.g., vibrations, pulses).

Lower-order thinking — involves one step or action and can include activities like observing, noting, categorizing, or recording.

Mediated emersion — allows students to work within an all-encompassing, digitally enhanced environment.

Metacognition — in short, thinking about thinking. It refers to students' consciousness of their own thinking and how they go about that thinking.

Physical simulations — are simulations' representations of systems or processes using objects or actions.

Process goals — focus on how knowledge and theories are generated within the domains.

Screen media — digital devices that often serve as input devices, such as touch screens. Screen media can be further divided into desktop and mobile hardware.

Universal design — understanding the goals for the simulation, the barriers to learning using this technology, the ways to overcome these barriers, and a mechanism to evaluate the accessibility of the simulation.

Virtual reality	applications are more immersive and are completely separated from a the real-world.
Whole body simulations	allow the user to create movement while learning about phenomena.

Endnotes

[1] Collins, A., & Halverson, R. (2009). *Rethinking education in the age of technology: The digital revolution and schooling in America.* Boston, MA: MITOpenCourseWare.

[2] Gee, J. P. (2008). Learning theory, video games, and popular culture. In K. Drotner & S. Livingstone (Eds.), *The international handbook of children, media, and culture* (pp. 196–211). Thousand Oaks, CA: Sage Publications Inc.

[3] National Center for Research in Vocational Education. (1977). Professional teacher education module series: Present information with filmstrips and slides, module C-24 of category C—instructional execution. Columbus, OH: Ohio State University.

[4] Bradley, P. (2006). The history of simulation in medical education and possible future directions. *Medical Education, 40*(3), 254–262.

[5] Cooper, J. B., & Taqueti, V. R. (2004). A brief history of the development of mannequin simulators for clinical education and training. *BMJ Quality & Safety, 13*(1), i11–i18.

[6] Gee, J. P. (2009). Games, learning, and 21st century survival skills. *Journal for Virtual Worlds Research, 2*(1).

[7] Lindgren, R., Tscholl, M., Wang, S., & Johnson, E. (2016). Enhancing learning and engagement through embodied interaction within a mixed reality simulation. *Computers & Education, 95*, 174–187.

[8] Wang, J. Y., Wu, H. K., & Hsu, Y. S. (2017). Using mobile applications for learning: Effects of simulation design, visual-motor integration, and spatial ability on high school students' conceptual understanding. *Computers in Human Behavior, 66*, 103–113.

[9] Squire, K., Barnett, M., Grant, J. M., & Higginbotham, T. (2004). *Electromagnetism supercharged! Learning physics with digital simulation games*. Paper presented at the Proceedings of the 6th international conference on Learning sciences, Santa Monica, CA.

[10] Dunleavy, M., Dede, C., & Mitchell, R. (2009). Affordances and limitations of immersive participatory augmented reality simulations for teaching and learning. *Journal of Science Education Technology, 18*(1), 7–22.

[11] Rubio-Tamayo, J., Gertrudix Barrio, M., & García García, F. (2017). Immersive environments and virtual reality: Systematic review and advances in communication, interaction and simulation. *Multimodal Technologies and Interaction, 1*(4), 21.

[12] Klopfer, E., Squire, K., & Jenkins, H. (2002). *Environmental detectives: PDAs as a window into a virtual simulated world*. Paper presented at the Wireless and Mobile Technologies in Education, 2002. Proceedings. IEEE International Workshop on Wireless and Mobile Technologies in Education, Tokushima, Japan.

[13] Frederking, B. (2005). Simulations and student learning. *Journal of Political Science Education, 1*(3), 385–393.

[14] Fraser, D., Pillay, R., Tjatindi, L., & Case, J. (2007). Enhancing the learning of fluid mechanics using computer simulations. *Journal of Engineering Education, 96*(4), 381–388.

[15] Halverson, R., & Steinkuehler, C. (2016). Games and learning. In C. Haythornthwaite, R. Andrews, J. Fransman, & E. M. Meyers (Eds.), *The Sage handbook of E-learning research* (2nd ed.). Washington, DC: Sage Publications Inc.

[16] Honey, M., & Hilton, M. (2011). *Committee on science learning: Computer games, simulations, and education. Learning science through computer games and simulations*. Washington, DC: National Academies Press.

[17] Scalise, K., Timms, M., Moorjani, A., Clark, L., Holtermann, K., & Irvin, P. S. (2011). Student learning in science simulations: Design features that promote learning gains. *Journal of Research in Science Teaching, 48*(9), 1050–1078.

[18] Bodemer, D., Ploetzner, R., Feuerlein, I., & Spada, H. (2004). The active integration of information during learning with dynamic and interactive visualisations. *Learning and Instruction, 14*(3), 325–341.

[19] Adams, W. K. (2010). Student engagement and learning with PhET interactive simulations. *Il Nuovo Cimento*, 1–12.

[20] Smetana, L. K., & Bell, R. L. (2012). Computer simulations to support science instruction and learning: A critical review of the literature. *International Journal of Science Education, 34*(9), 1337–1370.

[21] Miller, J. L., & Kocurek, C. A. (2017). Principles for educational game development for young children. *Journal of Children and Media, 11*(3), 314–329.

[22] De Freitas, S., & Oliver, M. (2006). How can exploratory learning with games and simulations within the curriculum be most effectively evaluated? *Computers & Education, 46*(3), 249–264.

[23] Barton, K., & Maharg, P. (2006). E-Simulations in the wild: Interdisciplinary research, design, & implementation. In D. Gibson, C. Aldrich, & M. Prensky (Eds.), *Games and simulations in online learning: Research & development frameworks* (pp. 115–149). Hershey, PA: Information Science Publishing.

[24] Vygotsky, L. (1978). Interaction between learning and development. *Readings on the Development of Children, 23*(3), 34–41.

[25] Piaget, J. (1964). Part I: Cognitive development in children: Piaget development and learning. *Journal of Research in Science Teaching, 2*(3), 176–186.

[26] Donovan, S., & Bransford, J. (2005). *How students learn*. Washington, DC: National Academies Press.

[27] Smith Iii, J. P., diSessa, A. A., & Roschelle, J. (1994). Misconceptions reconceived: A constructivist analysis of knowledge in transition. *Journal of the Learning Sciences, 3*(2), 115–163.

[28] Posner, G. J., Strike, K. A., Hewson, P. W., & Gertzog, W. A. (1982). Accommodation of a scientific conception: Toward a theory of conceptual change. *Science Education, 66*(2), 211–227.

[29] Elby, A., & Hammer, D. (2010). Epistemological resources and framing: A cognitive framework for helping teachers interpret and respond to their students' epistemologies. In L.

D. Bendixen & F. C. Feucht (Eds.), *Personal epistemology in the classroom: Theory, research, and implications for practice* (pp. 409–434). New York: Cambridge University Press.
[30] Gee, J. P. (2008). Learning and games. In K. Salen (Ed.), *The ecology of games: Connecting youth, games, learning and instruction* (Vol. 3, pp. 21–40). Cambridge, MA: MIT Press.
[31] Gee, J. P. (2003). What video games have to teach us about learning and literacy. *Computers in Entertainment, 1*(1), 1–4.
[32] Squire, K., & Barab, S. (2004). *Replaying history: Engaging urban underserved students in learning world history through computer simulation games.* Paper presented at the Proceedings of the 6th international conference on Learning sciences, Santa Monica, CA.
[33] Cantrell, P., Pekcan, G., Itani, A., & Velasquez-Bryant, N. (2006). The effects of engineering modules on student learning in middle school science classrooms. *Journal of Engineering Education, 95*(4), 301–309.
[34] Kolb, D. A. (1984). *Experience as the source of learning and development.* Upper Saddle River, NJ: Prentice Hall.
[35] Vos, L. (2015). Simulation games in business and marketing education: How educators assess student learning from simulations. *The International Journal of Management Education, 13*(1), 57–74.
[36] Lane, D. M., & Peres, S. C. (2006). *Interactive simulations in the teaching of statistics: Promise and pitfalls.* Paper presented at the Proceedings of the Seventh International Conference on Teaching Statistics, Voorburg, The Netherlands.
[37] Squire, K. (2006). From content to context: Videogames as designed experience. *Educational Researcher, 35*(8), 19–29.
[38] Squire, K. (2017). Innovation in times of uncertainty. *On the Horizon, 25*(4), 293–308.
[39] Rose, D. (2000). Universal design for learning. *Journal of Special Education Technology, 15*(3), 45–49.
[40] Athreya, B. H., & Mouza, C. (2017). *Thinking skills for the digital generation: The development of thinking and learning in the age of information.* Cham, Switzerland: Springer.

[41] Chaudron, S., Plowman, L., Beutel, M. E., Černikova, M., Donoso Navarette, V., Dreier, M., ... Wölfling, K. (2015). Young children (0–8) and digital technology—EU report. Luxembourg: Publications Office of the European Union.

[42] Rideout, V. (2014). *Learning at home: Families' educational media use in America.* Paper presented at the Joan Ganz Cooney Center at Sesame Workshop, New York.

[43] Lenhart, A., Duggan, M., Perrin, A., Stepler, R., Rainie, H., & Parker, K. (2015). *Teens, social media & technology overview 2015.* Pew Research Center [Internet & American Life Project], Washington, DC.

[44] Hourcade, J. P., Mascher, S. L., Wu, D., & Pantoja, L. (2015). Look, my baby is using an iPad! An analysis of YouTube videos of infants and toddlers using tablets. Paper presented at the Proceedings of the 33rd Annual ACM Conference on Human Factors in Computing Systems, Republic of Korea, Seoul.

[45] Radu, I., MacIntyre, B., & Lourenco, S. (2016). *Comparing children's crosshair and finger interactions in handheld augmented reality: Relationships between usability and child development.* Paper presented at the Proceedings of the The 15th International Conference on Interaction Design and Children, Manchester.

[46] Ni, Q., & Yu, Y. (2015). Research on educational mobile games and the effect it has on the cognitive development of preschool children. Paper presented at the 2015 Third International Conference on Digital Information, Networking, and Wireless Communications (DINWC), Moscow, Russia.

[47] Dinsmore, D. L., & Zoellner, B. P. (2018). The relation between cognitive and metacognitive strategic processing during a science simulation. *British Journal of Educational Psychology, 88*(1), 95–117.

[48] Alexander, P. A. (1997). Mapping the multidimensional nature of domain learning: The interplay of cognitive, motivational, and strategic forces. *Advances in Motivation and Achievement, 10,* 213–250.

[49] Schoenfeld, A. H. (1987). What's all the fuss about metacognition. *Cognitive Science and Mathematics Education, 189,* 215.

[50] D'Angelo, C., Rutstein, D., Harris, C., Bernard, R., Borokhovski, E., & Haertel, G. (2014). *Simulations for STEM*

learning: Systematic review and meta-analysis. Menlo Park: SRI International.

[51] Flick, L., & Bell, R. (2000). Preparing tomorrow's science teachers to use technology: Guidelines for science educators. *Contemporary Issues in Technology and Teacher Education, 1*(1), 39–60.

[52] National Governors Association Center for Best Practices & Council of Chief State School Officers. (2010). *Common core state standards*. Washington, DC: National Governors Association Center for Best Practices Council of Chief State School Officers.

[53] Alibali, M. W., & Nathan, M. J. (2012). Embodiment in mathematics teaching and learning: Evidence from learners' and teachers' gestures. *Journal of the Learning Sciences, 21*(2), 247–286.

[54] Van Eck, R., & Dempsey, J. (2002). The effect of competition and contextualized advisement on the transfer of mathematics skills a computer-based instructional simulation game. *Educational Technology Research and Development, 50*(3), 23–41.

[55] Steinkuehler, C., & Duncan, S. (2008). Scientific habits of mind in virtual worlds. *Journal of Science Education and Technology, 17*(6), 530–543.

[56] Rutherford, F. J., & Ahlgren, A. (1990). *Science for all Americans*. New York: Oxford University Press.

[57] National Research Council. (1996). *National science education standards*. Washington, DC: National Academies Press.

[58] American Association for the Advancement of Science. (1993). *Benchmarks for science literacy*. New York: Oxford University Press.

[59] National Research Council. (2012). *A framework for K-12 science education: Practices, crosscutting concepts, and core ideas*. Washington, DC: National Academies Press.

[60] Next Generation Science Standards Lead States. (2013). *Next generation science standards: For states, by states*. In Appendix D: All standards, all students: Making the next generation science standards accessible to all students. Washington, DC: National Academy Press.

[61] Bransford, J. D., Brown, A. L., & Cocking, R. R. (2000). *How people learn*. Washington, DC: National Academies Press.

[62] Dickes, A. C., Sengupta, P., Farris, A. V., & Basu, S. (2016). Development of mechanistic reasoning and multilevel

explanations of ecology in third grade using agent-based models. *Science Education*, *100*(4), 734–776.

[63] McClean, P., Johnson, C., Rogers, R., Daniels, L., Reber, J., Slator, M., ... White, A. (2005). Molecular and cellular biology animations: Development and impact on student learning. *Cell Biology Education*, *4*(2), 169–179.

[64] Calley, J., & Jungck, J. (1997). *Genetics construction kit* (The BioQUEST Library IV, version 1.1 B3) [Computer software]. College Park: The ePress Project.

[65] Cartier, J. L., Stewart, J., & Zoellner, B. (2006). Modeling and inquiry in a high school genetics class. *American Biology Teacher*, *68*(6), 334–340.

[66] National Council for the Social Studies. (2010). *National curriculum standards for social studies: A framework for teaching, learning, and assessment*. Silver Spring, MD: National Council for the Social Studies.

[67] Shellman, S. M., & Turan, K. (2006). Do simulations enhance student learning? An empirical evaluation of an IR simulation. *Journal of Political Science Education*, *2*(1), 19–32.

[68] Gottlieb, O, & Ash, J. (2013). *Jewish Time Jump: New York* [Video Game]. New York: ConverJent: Jewish Games for Learning.

[69] Gottlieb, O. (2018). Time travel, labour history, and the null curriculum: New design knowledge for mobile augmented reality history games. *International Journal of Heritage Studies*, *24*(3), 287–299.

[70] Barboza, D. (2010, June 6). After suicide, scrutiny of China's grim factories. *New York Times*. Retrieved from www.nytimes.com/2010/06/07/business/global/07suicide.html

[71] Schwartz, N. D., Cohen, P., & Hirschfeld Davis, J. (2017, July 27). Wisconsin's Lavish Lure for Foxconn: $3 billion in tax subsidies. *New York Times*. Retrieved from www.nytimes.com/2017/07/27/business/wisconsin-foxconn-tax-subsidies.html?searchResultPosition=6

[72] Squire, K. D., & Jan, M. (2007). Mad city mystery: Developing scientific argumentation skills with a place-based augmented reality game on handheld computers. *Journal of Science Education and Technology*, *16*(1), 5–29.

[73] Rudolph, J. L. (2002). *Scientists in the classroom: The cold war reconstruction of American science education* (1st ed.). New York: Palgave Macmillan.

Index

active learning 88–89, 112
Adams, W. K. 55, 116
Akwaaba Foundation 118
Alexander, P. A. 109
Alibali, M. W. 111
Alien Contact! 54, 109
All Quiet on the Western Front (Remarque) 10
Athreya, B. H. 64, 69
augmented reality applications: cognition and 75; contextual learning and 35; defining 14; inputs and 74; instructional support in 76; motor skills and 73; physical development and 70; student engagement in 53; student experiences and 17
authentic assessment 58–59

Barnett, M. 7, 33, 92
Basu, S. 114
Bejeweled 43
Bell, R. 101, 121
Bell, R. L. 49, 50, 51, 89
Benchmarks for Science Literacy 112
Beutel, M. 80
Bloom's taxonomy 89
Bodemer, D. 70, 95
Bring Your Own Device 22, 60
broader horizons 61

Call of Duty 45
Cantrell, P. 39
Case, J. 10, 49, 57
cell phones 67, 69
Chaudron, S. 80
Chauncey, H. 123
children *see* older students; young children
citizenship 60
Civilization 12
Clark, L. 16
C-LEARNS 91
cognition: conceptual understanding and 94–95; defining 89; embodied 111; goals in 90; higher-order thinking 89; lower-order thinking 89; schema and 31; simulations and 90–95, 99; strategies and 91–93, 99; synthesis and 93–94
cognitive development: active learning and 89; inputs and 75; nontraditional strategies in 76; simulation design and 77–79, 88; task demands and 75–76; technological skills and 80
cognitive load 55
cognitive processing 25
collaboration 58
Collins, A. 46–47, 60
Committee on Science Learning (National Research Council) 113
Common Core State Standards 20, 103, 107, 109–111

communities of practice 36–37, 58
conceptual learning: cognitive strategies and 94–95; engaged exploration in 55–56; existing conceptions in 37; first-hand experience in 33–34; game-based simulations and 48; goals in 30; larger context of 39; simulations and 62; student conceptual ecology in 31–32; worksheet use in 57
conceptual simulations 29
constructivist learning: cognition and 31; learning communities and 59; pedagogical approaches in 28; schema in 31; simulations in 28, 30–34, 37, 42; social/cultural 30
content goals 103–105
contextual learning 35
Cooney Center 68
Crystal Island 102
cues 94
curriculum: designed-experience approach 44–45; developmental issues in 77; higher-order outcomes 49; instructional support in 51; student support in 51–52; teacher use of simulations in 48–49, 121–124
customization 46

Dear Angelica 121
De Freitas, S. 24, 25
design-based thinking 45–46
designed experiences 44–45
Deus Ex 12
developmental levels: cognitive 75–80; complexity of representations and 65–66; digital games and 77–79; educational game design and 71–72, 80–82; input methods and 66, 74–75; literacy considerations and 80–82; older students 82–84; physical development and 69–70, 72–74; physical interface and 72–73; self-progress and 76; social interactions and 83; spatial ability and 83; subject matter and 66; technology practices and 67–72; young children 77–82, 84
Dickes, A. C. 114
diegesis 26
differentiated instruction 86–87
digital games: defining 11; developmental levels and 64, 77–79; equity in 85–86; learning goals and 20; representation of phenomena in 12–13; as simulations 12–13; 21st century skills and 27
digital generation 69
digital media 68, 71
digital simulations: augmented reality applications 14; conceptual space and 67; depth of content in 86; developmental issues in 64–87; differentiated instruction and 86–87; educator role in 122–124; guidelines for 121–122; hardware for 15–16; instructional support in 66, 94–95; interactive 3–5, 20; interfaces for 5; metacognitive strategies and 98–99; mixed reality applications 14–15; nontraditional cognitive strategies in 76; scientific

processes and 101; screen media 5–6; student interactions with 65; students with disabilities and 59–60; whole body 14–15; young children 77–82; *see also* simulations
Dinsmore, D. L. 91, 100
diversity 61
domain knowledge 104, 109
domain-specific frameworks: art and 121; connecting facts to 39–41; content/process goals in 103–106; digital simulations and 102–107; engineering problems 120; experience and 39–40; language arts learning goals 107–109; mathematics learning goals 109–112; phenomena and 39; science learning goals 112–116; social studies learning goals 117–120; STEM areas 121; student learning and 40
Donoso Navarrete, V. 80
Dow Day 120
Duncan, S. 111

educational games: communities of practice and 36–37; developmental levels and 71–72, 80–81; differentiated instruction and 87; equity and 61, 85–86; language arts learning goals and 108–109; play and 85; principles in application design 23–24; student engagement in 43–44; *see also* game-based simulations
educational research 125
educational technology: costs of 22–23; equity and 60–61; integrating into instruction 22–23; students with disabilities and 59–60; traditional schooling vs. 46–48; use of 2
Elby, A. 32
Elder Scrolls III, The 12
embodiment 5, 111
engaged exploration 55–56
engineering problems 10, 39–40, 56–57, 120
epistemological framing 32
equity 60–61, 85–86
existing conceptions 31, 37–38
experience 39–40, 44–45

Farris, A. V. 114
FeelReel virtual-reality device 8
Feuerlein, I. 70, 95
films 123–124
fixed devices 16
Flick, L. 101, 121
FoldIt 116
Framework for K-12 Science Education 112
Fraser, D. 10, 49, 57
Frederking, B. 10, 52
Full Spectrum Warrior 12

game-based simulations: conceptual understanding in 48; contextual learning and 36; effectiveness of 108; problem-solving in 11; representations of phenomena in 12–13; student understanding and 45–46; *see also* educational games
games *see* digital games; educational games
García García, F. 13, 108, 121
Gee, J. P. viii, 12, 27, 34, 36, 43, 45, 87
Genetics Construction Kit 115
Gertrudix Barrio, M. 13, 108, 121
gesture-controlled interfaces 6, 111

Gibson, D. 29
Global Positioning Systems (GPS) 8
Grant, J. M. 7, 33, 92
guided discovery methodology 50–51

Half-Life 12
Halverson, R. 11, 13, 46–47, 60, 108
Hammer, D. 32
hardware: Bring Your Own Device option 22, 60; fixed 16; input devices and 5, 70; physical interface and 70, 72–73; portable devices 16; simulations and 15–16
Higginbotham, T. 7, 33, 92
high-embodiment devices 5
higher-order outcomes 49
higher-order thinking 89
Hilton, M. 113
Holtermann, K. 16
Honey, M. 113
How Students Learn (National Research Council) 31
Hsu, Y. S. 55, 82

inductive reasoning 49
Infectious Ape 121
input devices 5, 70, 73
inquiry-based instruction 27, 61, 76
interactivity 3–6, 20
Internet 68
iPad 70
Irvin, P. S. 16
Itani, A. 39

Jenkins, H. 16
Jewish Time Jump: New York 119
Johnson, E. 5, 40, 53–54

kinematics 82
Klopfer, E. 16
Kocurek, C. A. 23–24, 61, 71, 73, 80, 82–83, 85

Lane, D. M. 43, 110
language arts learning goals 107–109
learner and classes 25
learning communities 59
learning frameworks: active approach to 35; conceptual 30–32, 37, 42, 56, 62; constructivist 28, 30–34, 37, 42; epistemological 32; inquiry-based 27, 61, 76; model-based 99; outcomes and 29–30; pedagogical approaches and 42–44; simulations and 29–30, 32–34, 61; traditional vs. technology 46–48; zone of proximal development and 30
learning outcomes: frameworks for 29–30; higher-order 49; instructional support in 62; scaffolding and 44, 62; simulations and 29; Universal Design and 59–60
Lindgren, R. 5, 40, 53–54
literacy considerations 80–82
Lourenco, S. 73, 79
low-embodiment devices 5
lower-order thinking 89

MacIntyre, B. 73, 79
mathematics learning goals 109–112
mediated emersion 8
mental models 45
metacognition: active learning and 89; defining 89; digital simulations and 97–99; game-based simulations and 45–46; goals in 95–96; instructional support in 95–97, 99–100; scaffolding and 95–96; simulation experience and 88–89; simulations and 21, 41–42, 90; strategies and 96–98; student learning and

31; teacher prompts and 33, 41
MEteor 14, 38, 53–54
Miller, J. L. 23–24, 61, 71, 73, 80, 82–83, 85
mixed reality applications 14–15
mobile devices 5–6, 67, 69
model-based instruction 99
Modeling for Understanding in Science Education 112
Moorjani, A. 16
motion sensors 6
motor skills 72–73
Mouza, C. 64, 69

Nathan, M. J. 111
National Council for Teachers of Mathematics Standards 103
National Council for the Social Studies 117
National Curriculum Standards for Social Studies 103, 117
National Research Council 12, 31, 99, 116
National Science Education Standards 112
Nature 116
Next Generation Science Standards 21, 99, 103, 112, 116
Ni, Q. 76–78
Norman, D. 78

older students 82–84
Oliver, M. 24, 25
online forums 111–112, 116
operational models 29–30

Partnership for 21st Century Skills 20
pedagogical approaches: blended models of 56; communities of practice and 58; constructivist learning and 28; deep engagement and 43–44; educational technology and 46–48; guided discovery methodology in 50–51; instructional support in 42–44, 49–53, 55–57, 62; nontraditional teaching and 43; place-based learning 118–120; simulation quality and 54–55; simulation strategies and 21; student understanding and 45–46; traditional 46–48; whole body simulations 53–54
Pekcan, G. 39
Peres, S. C. 43, 111
Personal Digital Assistants 16
Pew Research Center 69
phenomena: accessibility of 62; digital game representations of 12–13; domain-specific frameworks for 39; existing conceptions of 38; multiple representations of 86; simulations of 9–10, 28, 52; student manipulation of 19
PhET lab simulations 19, 55
physical development: inputs and 73–75; motor skills and 72–73; physical interface and 69–70; visual acuity and 73
physical simulations 3
Piaget, J. 31, 77
Pillay, R. 10, 49, 57
place-based learning 118–120
play 85
Ploetzner, R. 70, 95
portable devices 7–8, 16
Principles and Standards for School Mathematics 109–110
process goals 103, 105
professional development 23, 44

Radu, I. 73, 79
reflection 41–42, 76, 96
Remarque, Erich Maria 10
representational world 26
Resusci Anne Simulator 3
Rice Virtual Lab 110
Rise of Nations 12
Rubio-Tamayo, J. 13, 108, 121
Rudolph, J. L. 123

scaffolding: constructivist learning and 59; individuality and 16; instructional support in 84, 95–96; learning outcomes and 44, 62; metacognition and 95–96; on-screen features and 79; task demands and 76, 82; zone of proximal development and 30
Scalise, K. 16
schema 31
Schoenfeld, A. H. 96, 98
science education: conceptual frameworks for 31–32; digital simulations and 101; engaged exploration in 55–56; existing conceptions in 31; hands-on design in 39, 101; metacognition and 31; simulations and 39, 49; strategies and 100; technology guidelines for 121–122
Science for All Americans 112
science learning goals 112–116
screen media 5–6
screen time 84–85
self-progress 76
Sengupta, P. 114
settings 9
Shellman, S. M. 117–118
SimCity 11, 19
SIMPOLICON 75, 102, 118
Sims, The 12
simulated outputs 7–8
simulations: art and 121; authenticity and viii; conceptual models 29–30, 32, 34; curricular advantages of 18–21; engineering problems and 120; factors when choosing 21–22; frameworks for ix; functions of 8–9; game-based 11–12, 36; hardware for 15–16; integrating into instruction 22–23; interactivity and 20; language arts learning goals and 107–109; learning goals and 20–21; logistical advantages of 16–17; mathematics learning goals and 109–112; movement and 40–41; nature of 10–11; operational models 29–30; of phenomena 9–10, 19, 28, 38–39; physical 3; processes of learning and 24; science learning goals and 112–116; of settings 9; social studies learning goals and 117–120; STEM areas and 121; types of 3–4; use of vii, 1–2, 48–49; *see also* augmented reality applications; digital simulations; educational games; virtual reality applications
Smetana, L. K. 49, 50, 51, 89
social cohesion 60–61
social/cultural constructivism 30
social interactions 83–84
social learning 36
social mediation 84–85
social studies learning goals 117–120
Spada, H. 70, 95
spatial ability 83
special education students 39–40
Squire, K. 7, 16, 33, 44, 92
Steinkuehler, C. 11, 13, 46, 108, 111
STEM areas 121

student-centered simulations 21
student learning: cognitive load 55; conceptual understanding in 31, 56–57; contextual information and 35; curricular design for 34–35; domain-specific frameworks and 40; educational research and 125; existing conceptions and 37–38; focus in 49–50; interactive simulations and 20; interest in application functionality 52–53; processes of 24; self-progress in 76; simulations supporting 29, 34; social context and 36; teamwork in 58; technology practices and 67–69; through experience 34; whole body simulations 53–54; zone of proximal development and 30
students with disabilities 59–60
Supercharged 92, 98
SWAT IV 12

Teachers Integrating Engineering into Science (TIES) program 56, 120
teamwork 58
technology practices: cognitive challenges and 70–71; content and 67–68; physical development and 69–71; socioeconomic status and 69; students and 67–69
television 67–68, 71
Tetris 43
Tiltbrush 121
Timms, M. 16
Tjatindi, L. 10, 49, 57
touchscreens 5–6, 74–75, 83
traditional schooling 46–48
Trivial Pursuit 43

Tscholl, M. 5, 40, 53–54
Turan, K. 117–118
21st century skills 27

uniform learning 46
Universal Design 59–60

Valkyria Chronicles 45
Velasquez-Bryant, N. 39
Virtual Cell Animation Collection 114
Virtual City Planner 102, 107, 118
virtual reality applications: art and 121; defining 14; language arts learning goals and 108–109; mathematics learning goals and 111; as simulations 13–14
visual acuity 73
Vos, L. 41, 58, 114
Vygotsky, L. 30, 58

Wang, J. Y. 55, 82
Wang, S. 5, 40, 53–54
Webb's taxonomy 89
whole body simulations 14–15, 53–54
World of WarCraft 37
Wu, H. K. 55, 82

young children: creating games for 78–79; developmental levels and 77–78; digital simulations and 77–82; emotional goals 79; imitation and 78; instructional support in 85; interactive modes 78; literacy considerations and 80–82; prosocial behavior and 78; screen time and 84–85; social mediation and 84–85
Yu, Y. 76–78

Zoellner, B. P. 91, 100
zone of proximal development 30